TRUE TO LIFE

PRE-INTERMEDIATE

Ruth Gairns
Stuart Redman

CLASS BOOK

 CAMBRIDGE
UNIVERSITY PRESS

PUBLISHED BY THE PRESS SYNDICATE OF THE UNIVERSITY OF CAMBRIDGE
The Pitt Building, Trumpington Street, Cambridge, United Kingdom

CAMBRIDGE UNIVERSITY PRESS
The Edinburgh Building, Cambridge CB2 2RU, UK
40 West 20th Street, New York, NY 10011–4211, USA
477 Williamstown Road, Port Melbourne, VIC 3207, Australia
Ruiz de Alarcón 13, 28014 Madrid, Spain
Dock House, The Waterfront, Cape Town 8001, South Africa

http://www.cambridge.org

First published 1995
Eighth printing 2001

Printed in the United Kingdom at the University Press, Cambridge

ISBN 0 521 42145 4 Class Book
ISBN 0 521 42146 2 Personal Study Workbook
ISBN 0 521 42147 0 Teacher's Book
ISBN 0 521 42148 9 Class Cassette Set
ISBN 0 521 42149 7 Personal Study Workbook Cassette
ISBN 0 521 48575 4 Personal Study Workbook Audio CD

CONTENTS

COURSE OVERVIEW   4

1 **GETTING STARTED**   6

2 **ASKING QUESTIONS**   12

3 **STREETLIFE**   18

4 **CREATIVITY**   24

5 **YOU AND YOUR BODY**   30

6 **LEARNING – PAST AND PRESENT**   36

7 **LETTERS THAT TELL A STORY**   43

8 **TAKE IT OR LEAVE IT**   50

9 **FOOD AND DRINK**   57

10 **FEELINGS: THE GOOD, THE BAD AND THE UGLY**   63

11 **WEATHER**   70

12 **ROMANCE**   76

13 **IT'S BETTER TO TRAVEL THAN TO ARRIVE**   83

14 **POSSESSIONS**   89

15 **RULES**   95

16 **KEEPING THE CUSTOMER SATISFIED**   102

17 **PICTURE THIS!**   108

18 **LISTS**   114

19 **PUT YOUR TRUST IN OTHERS**   120

20 **THE SENSES**   127

21 **TIME**   133

22 **A SENSE OF HISTORY**   139

23 **WHOSE LIFE IS IT ANYWAY?**   145

24 **CINEMA AND THE ARTS**   151

GRAMMAR REFERENCE   158

ADDITIONAL MATERIAL   171

TAPESCRIPTS   173

IRREGULAR VERBS AND PHONETIC SYMBOLS   175

ACKNOWLEDGEMENTS   176

COURSE OVERVIEW

Unit	Language focus	Vocabulary	Topics	Review
1 GETTING STARTED	present simple and continuous different uses of *should* adverbs of degree	work and study routines office equipment adjectives for personality	work and study routines current activities learning English outside class	
2 ASKING QUESTIONS	forming questions past simple revision *how much* and *how many* *what's it like?* link words: *so, because,* *because of*	biographical information	asking personal questions grammar quiz talking about personal backgrounds	Unit 1
3 STREETLIFE	understanding and giving directions probability and possibility indirect questions	buildings and monuments roads and traffic prepositions	describing places finding your way questions people ask in the street	Unit 1 Unit 2
4 CREATIVITY	present perfect vs. past simple infinitive of purpose suggestions, refusals, apologies	creative verbs e.g. *paint, invent*	creativity tests creative experiences improvisation	Unit 2 Unit 3
5 YOU AND YOUR BODY	adverbs of frequency reflexive pronouns giving instructions	parts of the body verbs of movement time expressions health and fitness	health and fitness body stories DIY surgery	Unit 3 Unit 4
6 LEARNING – PAST AND PRESENT	present perfect vs. past simple (2) *before* and *after* + *-ing* spelling rules *so* and *such* use of *should*	school and education adjectives learning strategies	the adult classroom different ways of learning classroom behaviour	Unit 4 Unit 5
7 LETTERS THAT TELL A STORY	comparative and superlative adjectives *(don't) have to, (don't) need to* spelling	describing personality professions word building text types	handwriting analysis a short story	Unit 5 Unit 6

8 TAKE IT OR LEAVE IT	*going to* and *might* for future
	  plans
	present continuous for future
	  arrangements
	will for spontaneous decisions
		shopping
		phrasal verbs
		word building
			shopping
			grammar quiz
			paying for things
				Unit 6
				Unit 7

9 FOOD AND DRINK	present simple passive
	have to, don't have to, must,
	  mustn't, should, shouldn't
		food and drink
		restaurants
		cooking
			storing and preparing food
			drinks around the world
			eating customs and restaurants in
			  different cultures
				Unit 7
				Unit 8

10 FEELINGS: THE GOOD, THE BAD AND THE UGLY	verb + *-ing* or infinitive *could* for suggestions expressing feelings	emotions verb and noun collocation	personal likes, dislikes and regrets what makes you happy? how to beat a bad mood	Unit 8 Unit 9
11 WEATHER	*too* and *very* *enough* + noun and + adjective *too much, too many* quantifiers – *a bit, a lot* *can* to express known facts verb patterns	weather jobs consumer goods	reactions to the weather how climate affects jobs and the economy	Unit 9 Unit 10
12 ROMANCE	past continuous and past simple *when* and *while* verb + preposition	relationships and romance the countryside prepositional phrases	Valentine's Day writing verse extract from a short story holiday romances	Unit 10 Unit 11

Unit	Language focus	Vocabulary	Topics	Review
13 IT'S BETTER TO TRAVEL THAN TO ARRIVE	plural nouns countable and uncountable nouns requests and enquiries	airports and flying verb and noun collocation: travel	are you an organised traveller? quiz about air travel travellers' language problems	Unit 11 Unit 12
14 POSSESSIONS	present perfect vs. past simple (3) *for* and *since* *how long?*	possessions superordinates e.g. *pets,* *jewellery* household objects/appliances	your most important possessions explaining unusual situations matching people and possessions	Unit 12 Unit 13
15 RULES	*if* sentences with present tenses use of articles past obligation/permission	social behaviour geographical features verb and noun collocation	social customs in different cultures grammar rules school rules in different cultures	Unit 13 Unit 14
16 KEEPING THE CUSTOMER SATISFIED	*will, may* and *might* for predictions *if* sentences	money and business prefixes and word building character adjectives	customer service questionnaire good and bad service the consequences of radical changes young or old – who are the best employees?	Unit 14 Unit 15
17 PICTURE THIS!	link words: *so that, otherwise* *look* + adjective, *look like* + noun *could (be)* for speculation advice and warnings sequencing: *first of all, secondly*	photography interiors of rooms	taking good photographs making a complaint	Unit 15 Unit 16
18 LISTS	telephoning requests, suggestions, arrangements	crime vocabulary record keeping fixed phrases	making lists lists in language learning telephoning	Unit 16 Unit 17
19 PUT YOUR TRUST IN OTHERS	*if* sentences with *will, would* and *might* offers and requests	adjectives ending in *-ed* and *-ing* speech acts e.g. *agree,* *complain* guessing words in context	a short story about trust requests from a neighbour judging people on appearance	Unit 17 Unit 18
20 THE SENSES	*so* and *neither* *will, might, won't* for predictions *it sounds, smells, tastes like* …	likes and dislikes food, materials, nationalities technology	touch, taste and smell smells in different cultures identifying 20th century sounds changing technology perfume	Unit 18 Unit 19
21 TIME	*used to* + verb time clauses: *when, as soon as* tense revision	dates and numbers time expressions	a new calendar life changes time game	Unit 19 Unit 20
22 A SENSE OF HISTORY	past simple passive relative clauses: *who, which* link words: *although, however* *remember* + *-ing*	historical events	historical events children's interpretation of history telling fact from fiction	Unit 20 Unit 21
23 WHOSE LIFE IS IT ANYWAY?	adjectives and adverbs expressing preferences	everyday activities word building names and naming	choices in daily life choosing names for people choosing a partner	Unit 21 Unit 22
24 CINEMA AND THE ARTS	present simple active and passive past simple active and passive present perfect simple *be able to* + infinitive *good at* + *-ing*	cinema, theatre, music artistic professions adjectives describing character	qualities needed for creative jobs cinema and the Oscars entertainment in different cultures	Unit 22 Unit 23

GETTING STARTED

Language focus:
present simple and continuous
different uses of *should*
adverbs of degree

Vocabulary:
describing how we work and study
office equipment

1 Think about learning English in class and outside class. How often do you do these things?

speak in English
read something in English
see a film or TV programme in English
write something in English
use an English dictionary

Discuss in groups.

2 Answer the questionnaire by circling the correct answer. If none of the answers is correct, write your own answer in (d).

1. When you work or study at home, do you do it:
   a. in the lounge?
   b. in a study?
   c. in your bedroom?
   d. ....

2. When you study at home, do you:
   a. sit at a desk?
   b. sit in an armchair?
   c. sit or lie on the floor?
   d. ....

3. Do you like to study:
   a. alone and in complete silence?
   b. alone but with background music?
   c. with others you can talk to?
   d. ....

4. Do you mostly write:
   a. with a pencil?
   b. with a ballpoint pen?
   c. on a word processor?
   d. ....

5. Do you prefer to study:
   a. early in the morning?
   b. in the afternoon?
   c. late at night?
   d. ....

6. Do you study:
   a. with a fixed routine?
   b. when you feel like it?
   c. only when you have to?
   d. ....

7. When you study, do you work:
   a. for 20–30 minutes and then have a break?
   b. for about an hour and then have a break?
   c. for long periods without interruptions?
   d. ....

8. When you study, do you:
   a. smoke a lot?
   b. drink a lot?
   c. eat a lot?
   d. ....

9. When you study, is your place of work:
   a. neat and tidy?
   b. a bit untidy, but you know where everything is?
   c. a mess?
   d. ....

10. When you concentrate, do you:
   a. bite your nails or the end of your pencil?
   b. scratch your head?
   c. tap your foot on the floor?
   d. ....

Work with a partner. Tell each other your answers.

3 How do you work? How does your partner work? Choose words from the box and any others necessary. Discuss your answers.

Example: *I'm a bit lazy. Cristina is very tidy.*

+	quite very	organised/efficient/tidy/hardworking
−	a bit quite very	disorganised/inefficient/untidy/lazy

4 ▭▭ ▭▭ The double ▭▭ here and in other parts of the book means that there are two recordings of the listening: an easier one, and a more difficult one. Decide which one to listen to, or listen to both.

Look at the questionnaire in Exercise 2 again. As you listen tick (✓) the answers the speaker gives. Compare your answers with a partner.

1 Do you know any of the books of Jeffrey Archer and Sally Beauman? What kind of books do they write, or do you think they write?

2 Look at the picture. Can you name all the things on the desk? Use a dictionary and work with a partner.

3 Work with a partner. One of you reads about Jeffrey, the other reads about Sally.

Jeffrey Archer

I don't want anything on my desk which is unnecessary. The pencils are in their place to my right, the sharpener is next to them and the script is in the centre. Simplicity is the secret for me, so all I've got on my desk apart from the phone, the clock, and of course a family photo, is my work.

I like felt-tip pens. At the moment, I'm writing the first draft of a new book. As always, I put out seven pens a week to the right of my script, and I use one a day and throw it away at the end of the day. These are silly things, but they are all part of making it easy. I even have an electric pencil sharpener so that I can't complain that I had to waste time sharpening a pencil.

Before I go to bed at night, I check that the table is perfect for the following morning, so that when I walk in the door at 7.00, everything is there. There is no excuse for me not to work apart from my own laziness.

Sally Beauman

I like to go into my office and shut the door with coffee and cigarettes and start by about 9.00. I always start in the same way – by re-reading yesterday's work. On the left-hand side of the desk I keep the pages of that day's work, and on a notepad, I make lots of notes and doodles and drawings with arrows and stars everywhere.

I work on an old Adler typewriter which was the machine I used when I was a journalist. I'm not very good at looking after it and it does get dusty and dirty, but I'm very fond of it. I'm learning to use a word processor, but I don't like it as much.

I like to work in a mess, so there is always a lot of stuff on the desk; correspondence, ashtray, coffee mugs, etc. A clean desk gives me no protection against the blank sheet of paper I have to write on.

4 On the desk in the photograph, Jeffrey and Sally's possessions are mixed up. With your partner, decide which desk the objects should be on:

Examples: *The typewriter should be on Sally's desk.*
The photo should be on Jeffrey's desk.

5 How do you organise the place where you study or work? Tell a partner and give as much information as possible.

Example: *My desk is a mess – I always have a lot of books on it and usually there are pens and pencils, and some empty coffee cups ...*

6 Look at these four sentences from the text. What tenses are used, and why?

I *work* on an old Adler typewriter.
Before I *go* to bed at night, I *check* that the table is perfect.
At the moment, I'*m writing* the first draft of a new book.
I'*m learning* to use a word processor, but I don't like it as much.

Compare your answers with others.

AT THE MOMENT I'M ...   present continuous; simple vs. continuous

1 Look at the pictures. What's happening? Use the vocabulary from the table in Exercise 3 on the next page to make sentences with a partner.

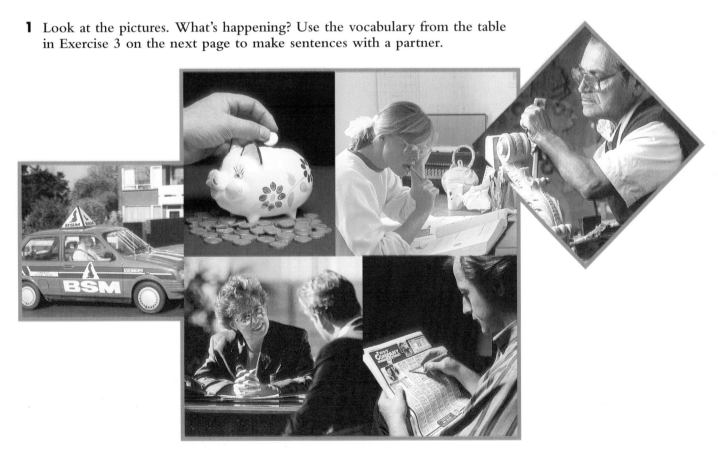

Do these activities happen over a very long period of time or not?

2 ▭ Listen to the recording. You will hear three people talking about exams and tests they are preparing for. Listen and answer these questions.

1. What exam/test is each person preparing for?
2. How does each person feel about it?

3 In groups, talk about the things in this table. Is anyone doing any of these things? And if so, why?

Who? Why?

1. Revising for an exam
2. Saving up for something
3. Looking for a new partner
4. Reading a serious book
5. Working hard
6. Making something
7. Changing jobs
8. Learning to drive

4 Now make some false sentences from the information you have.

Examples: *Mario is saving up for a ~~car~~.* holiday in China

~~Keiko~~ is trying to find a job. Ingrid

Read out your sentences. See who can correct them first.

5 Simple or continuous? Choose the best ending (a–j) for each of the sentence beginnings on the left.

Compare your answers with a partner.

1. I work for my father
2. I'm working for my father
3. I study
4. I'm studying
5. I do
6. I'm doing
7. I paint my room
8. I'm painting my room
9. I use a pen
10. I'm using a pen

a. for an important exam.
b. a typing course at the moment.
c. for all personal letters.
d. in his factory.
e. but I normally write in pencil.
f. dark blue.
g. until I find another job.
h. every evening after dinner.
i. the washing-up at weekends.
j. once every two or three years.

6 Look at the different uses of the present simple and the present continuous in the Grammar Reference on page 158. Which uses did you see in Exercise 5?

SPEAKING PARTNERS
English outside class; should

1 Juan and Ana are both Spanish, and they are studying English in Madrid where they have lessons three times a week. They want to practise speaking English outside class as well, so they meet in their free time and spend an hour practising together.

What problems do you think they have? Discuss with a partner, then tell the class.

Example: *They can't think what to talk about.*

2  Jackie (who is English) decided to find a speaking partner when she started learning Spanish in England.

Listen to her and make notes in the table below.

Problems	Solutions
1. *They didn't know what to talk about.*	
2.	
3.	
4.	

What advice can you give Juan and Ana?

Example: *They should talk about their homework together.*

3 Find a speaking partner in your class. First answer these questions about yourself.

1. Where do you live? If you live in a city, which district?
2. When are you free?
3. How often would you like to practise speaking English?
4. How long would you like to practise each time?
5. Where can you meet?

Move round the class and find one or two people who have answers similar to yours.

Agree to meet at a certain time in a certain place, to do the first speaking partners exercise on page 8 of your Personal Study Workbook.

PERSONAL STUDY WORKBOOK

In your Personal Study Workbook, you will find more exercises to help you with your learning. For Unit 1, these include:

- exercises on the present simple and present continuous
- an exercise on important classroom vocabulary
- listening to correct a text
- your first speaking partners activity
- the first page of your visual dictionary – office furniture and equipment
- writing about yourself

ASKING QUESTIONS

Language focus:
forming questions
past simple revision
how much and *how many*
what's it like?
link words: *so, because, because of*

Vocabulary:
biographical information

1 Think of some questions you would like to ask other people in the class.

Examples: *Tomoko, where did you get those earrings?*
            Mario, why do you often arrive late for class?
            What kind of car have you got, Ali?

Move round the class and ask your questions. If someone asks you a question you don't want to answer, you can say 'I'd rather not answer that', or 'I'd rather not say'.

2 Work in small groups. Study this list of questions. If there are words you don't know, you can:

a. try to guess the meaning
b. use a dictionary
c. ask other people in the group
d. ask your teacher

1. How much do you earn?
2. Are people in your profession well-paid?
3. Are you married? *or* Have you got a girlfriend/boyfriend/partner at the moment?
4. Are you happily married?
5. How old are you?
6. Who do you vote for?
7. Are you interested in politics?
8. Have you got any children?
9. Are you planning to have any children?
10. How much do you spend each month?
11. What does your partner do?
12. How much did your house/flat cost? *or* What is the rent on your house?
13. Are houses/flats expensive in the area where you live?
14. What does your partner look like?
15. Have you got any photos of your partner?

What does your partner look like?

Divide the questions into the three groups below, and then think of one more question for each group.

Money	Relationships	You
....	....	....
....	....	....
....	....	....
....	....	....
....	....	....
....	....	....
....	....	....

3 In your group, decide which of the questions in Exercise 2 you could ask these people: your closest friend; someone you know quite well; someone you met five minutes ago. You can use these phrases.

It's
rude
shocking
perfectly OK
to ask people, 'How much do you earn?'

4 Move round the class and ask people some of the questions in Exercise 2 and include some questions of your own. Remember that you don't have to answer if you don't want to.

How much do you earn?

Are people in your profession well-paid?

I'm sorry, I'd rather not say.

Are you interested in politics?

Are you married?

Yes, I am.

1 Try this quiz. Work with a partner.

1. The following questions are all incorrect.
   Correct them, and put your answers in the table.

   Where you live?
   What means 'cheat'?
   How often you went there?

Question word	Auxiliary verb	Subject	Main verb	....
....	....	....	....	....
....	....	....	....	....
....	....	....	....	....
....	....	....	....	....
....	....	....	....	....

2. These questions are also incorrect.
   Correct them, and put your answers in the table.

   Why you don't visit them?
   Why she didn't leave?

3. It is incorrect to say *Do you know where is the station?*. What is the correct question here?

   Do you know ....?

4. Write down three examples to show the difference between
   How much and *How many*.

   How much ....?   *How many* ....?
   ....?   ....?
   ....?   ....?

5. Write answers to these questions to show the difference in meaning.

   What's she like?   ....
   What does she like?   ....

6. Can you think of two different words that could be used instead of 'type' in the following question?

   What type of building is it?

   ....
   ....

7. Find the mistake in this dialogue and correct it.

   A: *Do you like classical music?*
   B: *Yes, very much.*
   A: *Well in that case, do you like to go to a concert tonight?*
   B: *Yes, I'd love to.*

8. When do we say *How do you do?* and when do we say *How are you?*

Check your answers to questions 1–3 using the Grammar Reference 1 and 2 on pages 158 and 159. Check the other answers with your teacher.

2 Here are some answers. What are the questions? Work with a partner and use phrases and question forms from the quiz in Exercise 1.

1. A: ....?
   B: No, thanks.

2. A: ....?
   B: I've no idea. Look it up in a dictionary.

3. A: ....?
   B: It's an IBM.

4. A: ....?
   B: Yes, it's down there on the right.

5. A: ....?
   B: Because I didn't know.

6. A: ....?
   B: About £20.

7. A: ....?
   B: About 20, including the teacher.

8. A: ....?
   B: Fine, thanks. And you?

9. A: ....?
   B: It's quite small, but the kitchen is very nice.

10. A: ....?
    B: Oh, about three times a week.

Practise the dialogues with a partner, then ask your partner three more questions about their home or work or family.

Example: *What's your room/flat like?*

ASKING ABOUT PERSONAL HISTORIES

link words; past simple

1 Look at these examples:

*I left school **because** I failed my exams. (reason)*
*I left school **because of** my poor exam results. (reason)*
*I failed my exams, **so** I left school. (consequence)*

When do we use *because* and when do we use *because of*?

Discuss with a partner.

2 Complete the sentence beginnings with a partner.

I lost my job because ....
I lost my job because of ....
I lost my job, so ....
It was difficult to get another job because ....
It was difficult to get another job because of ....
It was difficult to get another job, so ....

Tell the class your sentences.

3 Put these lines in the correct order. They are about a man called Paul.

At school I didn't do very well
and that is where I grew up.
because of my experience in Kenya.
and I failed most of my exams,
1 I was born in a small village,
so I decided to go abroad
When I came back to England a year later
so I left at the first opportunity.
and I got a job in a safari park near Nairobi.
I managed to get a job in a zoo near London
2 but we moved to Bristol when I was three
Unfortunately I couldn't find a job in England,

Compare your answers with a partner.
Which sentences relate to the pictures?

4 🔲🔲 Listen to the woman on the recording and answer these questions about her.

1. Where was she born?
2. Where did she grow up?
3. How did she do at school?
4. Did she pass all her exams?
5. When did she leave school?
6. What did she do after that?
7. What did she study there?
8. Where did she meet her husband?
9. Where is her husband from?
10. Where does she live now?

This woman is related to Paul. What is their relationship? Talk to a partner.

5 Now interview each other about your backgrounds. Use the questions above and any others you want to ask. Remember you do not have to answer if you don't want to.

PERSONAL STUDY WORKBOOK

In your Personal Study Workbook, you will find more exercises to help you with your learning. For Unit 2, these include:

- further exercises to practise questions
- a dictation followed by pronunciation practice
- a vocabulary exercise on synonyms and link words
- reading and listening about kangaroos
- writing a short autobiography

REVIEW OF UNIT 1

1 Describing pictures | present continuous |

A The pictures are all taken from advertisements.
Write down what the people are doing in each one, and what
you think they are advertising. Compare with a partner.

1
2
3
4
5

B ▭ Now listen to some English speakers talking about the advertisements. What
are the correct answers?

2 I often bite my nails | vocabulary: collocation |

A Fill the gaps with words from the box.

vote	lie	make	cheat	complain
waste	do	throw away	play	bite

1. I always .... my homework.
2. I don't .... cards very often.
3. I often .... my nails.
4. I sometimes .... in exams.
5. I often .... in cafés if the food is bad.

6. I always .... in national elections.
7. I often .... on the floor.
8. I never .... mistakes in class.
9. I never .... my time.
10. I never .... personal letters.

B Are these sentences true of you? If not, change them so they are true and then
discuss them in groups.

       sometimes
Example: *I ~~always~~ do my homework.*

3 Listen and answer | vocabulary |

▭ Listen to the questions and write your answers.

Compare your answers with a partner and then look at Tapescript 1 on page 173.

Tell your partner to close their book and then read the questions to them. How many
questions can they answer now?

STREETLIFE

Language focus:	Vocabulary:
understanding and giving directions	buildings and monuments
expressing probability and possibility	roads and traffic
indirect questions	

1 Match the words and pictures. Compare your answers with a partner.

1. statue
2. fountain
3. castle
4. mosque
5. cathedral
6. factory
7. high-rise building
8. road sign
9. souvenir shop
10. pedestrian crossing
11. parking meter
12. pavement café
13. litter bin
14. traffic lights
15. underground station

2 Work with the same partner. Answer these questions.

1. How do you pronounce the first six words in Exercise 1?
2. Where is the main stress on the other words in Exercise 1?

Now cover the words and test each other using the pictures. Pay careful attention to your pronunciation.

3 How many of the things in Exercise 1 will you find in these places? Make sentences, using the expressions below.

Budapest, Hungary

Parati Old Town, Brazil

There's definitely a … in …	There are definitely some …
There's probably a …	There are probably some …
There might be a …	There might be some …
There probably isn't a …	There probably aren't any …
There definitely isn't a …	There definitely aren't any …

4 Work with a partner. Imagine you are standing in a place you both know well. Write a description together of what you can see, but don't say where it is.

Example: *From where we are standing, we can see lots of parking meters, and there is a church on the left and two pavement cafés. The road is quite busy and there is a pedestrian crossing in front of us. In the distance there is a fountain with a statue in the middle of it.*

Read your description to another pair. Can they tell you where you are standing?

FINDING YOUR WAY
directions

1 Discuss these questions in small groups.

1. Are you good at finding your way? (on foot? in the car?)
2. Do you find it easy to give directions to people in your own language?
3. Do you ever get lost? If so, when was the last time?

2 Look at the map and find examples of 'ST'. What are the two different meanings of this abbreviation?

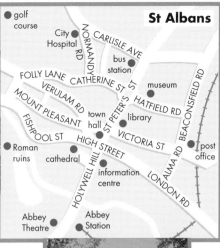

3 These directions will take you from Abbey Station to City Hospital. Use the map to put them in the correct order, and then compare with a partner.

keep going until you come to a roundabout
1 come out of Abbey Station
take the second turning on the right into Normandy Rd
go up Holywell Hill until you get to the High St
turn left at the roundabout
the hospital is at the end of the road on the left-hand side
go straight on, past the town hall

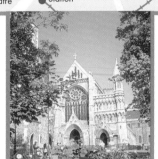

Practise these directions with your partner until you can say them without looking.

4 ☐☐ ☐☐ James travelled from London to visit a friend in City Hospital, and arrived at Abbey Station. Listen to what happened after that and draw his route on your map.

5 With a partner, make a list of useful phrases for giving directions from Exercise 3, and Tapescript 2 on page 173 and any others you know.

Examples: *turn left/right (at) …*
(after) …
(into) …

6 Draw a small map of your local area, and mark your house or flat on it, as in this example:

Give the map to a partner and give them directions from your house to different places or buildings on the map. Your partner must mark these places correctly.

STREET-WISE?   indirect questions

1 In your country, why do strangers stop you in the street and ask you questions? Continue this list with as many examples as you can.

Examples: *to ask you for money*
to ask you where you bought the jacket/hat/shoes you are wearing

Compare your answers in small groups.

2 Read this text about Rio de Janeiro. Underline the situations which are different from your own list. Then compare your answers.

Guil lives in Rio.

This is what he says about questions people ask him in the street.

" In Rio, people often stop you and ask you for directions, and the next most common thing people ask you for is a cigarette or a light. Then of course, there are people doing market research and they ask you if you'd like to try a product, like some new ice cream, and after that you have to answer questions about where you live, what your job is, etc. A lot of the time, people ask for money; you often get a mother with a couple of children who's asking for money for food for the children. Some people just come up to you in public transport and they ask you to buy things, maybe a small bag of oranges or chewing gum. And finally, men ask young women questions, like, 'Aren't you Luis's sister? Don't I know you?' "

3 Now look at the pictures. Who is asking what? With a partner, write down one or two questions for each picture.

Example: *In picture 1, possible questions for the man are:*
        'Do you know where the nearest paper shop is?'
        or
        'Excuse me. Is this the right way to the station?'

Compare your questions in groups.

1

2

3

4

5

6

4 ▭ Listen to people asking questions in similar situations. If the questions are different from yours, write them down.

5 Look at the first question again:

Do you know *where* the nearest paper shop *is*?

Why does the speaker use this indirect question, and not the direct question:

Where is the nearest paper shop?

Work with a partner. One of you says the beginning of the question, the other has to finish it in a suitable way.

Example: A: *Can you tell me when …*
B: *… the film starts?*
A: *Do you know where …*
B: *… my glasses are?*

Can you tell me when …?   Do you know how far …?
Do you know where …?   Can you tell me how much …?
Could you tell me what time …?   Do you know why …?

Work with a new partner. Ask them the complete questions and listen to their answers.

6 With a partner, choose your own street situation and develop a short conversation between two strangers.

PERSONAL STUDY WORKBOOK

In your Personal Study Workbook, you will find more exercises to help you with your learning. For Unit 3, these include:

- exercises on asking for and giving directions
- expressing possibility and probability
- a reading text about interesting and unusual maps
- a picture dictation for vocabulary and listening practice
- a speaking partners activity
- another page of your visual dictionary to complete – prepositions

---

REVIEW AND DEVELOPMENT

REVIEW OF UNIT 1

1 I'm quite hardworking   adjectives

Complete the grid with suitable opposites and then check your answers with your teacher.

hardworking	x	x	x	x	x	lazy
tidy	x	x	x	x	x	....
....	x	x	x	x	x	easy-going
organised	x	x	x	x	x	....
sensible	x	x	x	x	x	....
efficient	x	x	x	x	x	....

Where would you put yourself on each line of the grid? Put a circle round one x on each line and then compare your answers in groups.

2 Changing a habit   present simple and present continuous

Complete the sentences using the correct tenses and then compare your answers with a partner.

Example: *I usually work on an old typewriter but at the moment* **I'm writing by hand** *because* **my typewriter is broken.**

1. I usually study in the library but at the moment .... because
   ....
2. Generally .... but at the moment I'm not reading anything at all because ....
3. I normally go to the gym twice a week but at the moment .... because ....
4. Normally I .... but at the moment I'm doing it every day because my mother is ill.
5. I usually drive to work but at the moment .... because
   ....
6. Generally I .... but at the moment I'm practising five hours a day because I've got a concert soon.

With a partner, write two more complete sentences using the present simple and present continuous. Then tell the rest of the class.

REVIEW OF UNIT 2

1 What questions do you ask?   question practice

Which of the following questions do you *personally* use in your own country in your own language? Put them in order of frequency and compare your answers in groups.

1. Have you got a light?
2. How are you?
3. How do you do?
4. Do you take sugar?
5. What sort of car have you got?
6. Can I borrow your dictionary?
7. How do you pronounce …?
8. What's their flat like?
9. What does this word mean?
10. Do you know where my glasses are?

Work with your partner and think of another five questions that you need when you speak English.

2 Contractions and weak forms   pronunciation; dictation

A ⊂⊃ We often use contractions in English. Listen to these examples.

Examples: *Where do you live?* (pronounced 'd'you')
          What's the time?
          Haven't you got any money?

Sometimes the auxiliary verb is 'weak' and difficult to hear.
Listen to these examples.

Examples: *What are you doing?*   *What have you got in your bag?*
          When does he work?   *Where do they live?*

Now listen and write down these questions. At the end check your answers first with a partner and then with Tapescript 3 on page 173.

B Ask each other the questions and answer them. Pay attention to the pronunciation of the contractions and weak forms.

4

CREATIVITY

Language focus:
present perfect vs. past simple (1)
infinitive of purpose
suggestions, refusals, apologies

Vocabulary:
creative acts, e.g. paint, invent
describing speech acts,
e.g. suggest, refuse

vocabulary; infinitive of purpose

1 Read through the five tests. Then, with a partner, choose three and do them. (You may need to use a dictionary to help you with the vocabulary.)

TEST 1 Unusual Uses

Here are some things you can do with a brick:
You can use it to break a window.
You can use it to hold a door open.
You can use it as a weapon.
You can use it as a paperweight.

Now think of unusual uses for these:

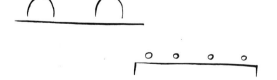

a knife

a newspaper

TEST 2 Patterns

Look at the geometric forms below. What could they be?
Make a list of possible answers for each picture.

TEST 3 Word Association

Look at the different meanings of *class*.
Now write as many meanings as possible for each of these words: light
back

a group of learners or students
a lesson (English class)

class

a social group
(middle class, working class,
upper class)

Services
(first class, economy class,
club class)

TEST 4 Story Endings

Read this story about an old married couple.

Joe was 84 and couldn't walk any more. His wife, Moira, looked after him. One day, two men came to the house and said they were from the electricity company. They wanted to check the electrical wiring. Moira let them in, and then went back to look after Joe. Later, she went into the kitchen and found one of the men holding her handbag.

Now complete the story in three different ways:
a. with a strange ending
b. with a sad ending
c. with a happy ending.

TEST 5 Lateral Thinking

There is a bowl of water on a table. You must not damage the bowl or move it. Think of as many ways as possible to get the water out of the bowl.

2 Work in small groups. Discuss these questions.

1. Which tests were easy, and why?
2. Which tests were difficult, and why?
3. Which is the best test of creativity? Can you think of a better test?

3 🔲🔲 Listen to two different endings for Test 4 – Story Endings. Are they strange, sad or happy?

YOUR CREATIVE EXPERIENCES   present perfect

1 Check you understand the vocabulary in this exercise, then discuss in small groups.

Is it easier to …
  – write a poem, or write an article for a newspaper or magazine?
  – invent a game, or invent a new dish (to eat)?
  – make an ornament, or make a poster?
  – paint a self-portrait, or draw a cartoon?
  – act in a play, or dance in front of an audience?
  – make a present for someone, or make a speech?
  – build something out of wood, or make something from paper?
  – design the decor of a room, or design something to wear?
  – compose a piece of music, or write the words for a song?

2 📖 Listen and write down the first two questions and answers in this space.

A: ....?

B: ....

A: ....?

C: ....

These questions are in the present perfect tense (*have* + past participle), because here we are talking about an event in the period of time from the past up to now. We don't know when the event happened.

📖 Now listen and write down the next two conversations on the recording.

A: ....?

D: ....

A: ....?

E: ....

What tense do D and E use, and why?

3 Has your teacher ever done any of the things in Exercise 1? Find out. Ask questions like this and listen carefully to the tenses in the answers. Before you begin, make sure you know the past participle of any irregular verbs (see page 175).

Examples: *Have you ever painted a self-portrait?*
Have you ever written a poem?

Have you ever painted a self-portrait?

4 What have you done in *your* life? Move round the class asking questions like the ones you asked your teacher. Add some questions of your own, if you like.

1 Read the dialogue and check that you understand it.
Then practise it with a partner.

(Doorbell rings. Lucy answers it.)

LUCY: Mark!
MARK: Hi, Lucy.
LUCY: Well, come on in.
MARK: Thanks. Hope I'm not late.
LUCY: Late?
MARK: Well, we did say tonight
        for dinner, didn't we?
LUCY: ...

2 ▭ Listen to this dialogue improvised by two pairs of actors. What happens at the end
of each one?

3 ▭ Now listen again. Does each sentence below describe something in the first
dialogue or the second?

Mark makes a suggestion.
Lucy is angry.
Mark apologises.
Lucy is in a panic.
Mark sounds a bit negative.
Mark refuses to help.
Mark is embarrassed.
Lucy is pleased to see Mark.

4 Match the phrases below with these categories: apologies suggestions refusals.

I'm terribly sorry.
How about going out for a meal?
I'm sorry, but that's just not possible.
Perhaps we could have dinner together.
I'm sorry, I can't.
Why don't we meet some other time?
I'd love to, but I'm afraid I can't.
Sorry to keep you waiting.

5 Work with a partner. Improvise the dialogue in Exercise 1 yourselves.

6 Now try improvising this dialogue with your partner.

(Front door opens. A arrives home.)

A: Hello, B.
B: Hi.
A: Guess what I've got.
B: What?
A: Tickets for the opera.
B: Brilliant! When?
A: Well, tonight of course.
B: …

📼 Listen to two actors improvising the dialogue. Is it very different from yours?

PERSONAL STUDY WORKBOOK

In your Personal Study Workbook, you will find more exercises to help you with your learning. For Unit 4, these include:

- further exercises and a dictation on the present perfect and past simple
- more creativity tests and a vocabulary game
- a reading passage about the way we think
- a vocabulary exercise on expressing personal feelings
- a creative listening task

REVIEW AND DEVELOPMENT

REVIEW OF UNIT 2

1 Got a light? | auxiliary verbs in questions |

A Sometimes when people ask questions in English, the auxiliary verb and pronoun are omitted.

Example: *Ready? = Are you ready?*

What words are omitted in these questions?

1. Coming?
2. Got a light?
3. Want a coffee?
4. Like a cigarette?
5. Have a good journey?
6. Ever been there?
7. Yours?
8. Get what you wanted?
9. Finished?
10. Tired?

B Find the best answer to each question from the following.

a. Sorry, I don't smoke.
b. Yes, almost.
c. No, it was absolutely terrible.
d. No, thanks.
e. No, I'm afraid I didn't.
f. Oh, yes, please. Just a small one.
g. No, I haven't.
h. No, not mine.
i. Yes, hang on a minute.
j. Yes, a bit.

C Ask a partner the full questions in Exercise A. See if they can reply quickly with the correct answers from Exercise B.

2 The teacher's shoes | question practice |

A Work with a partner. Write down fifteen questions to ask your teacher about his/her shoes. When you are ready you can ask your questions and your teacher will answer them and correct any mistakes.

Examples: *Where did you buy them?*
Do you often wear them?
Do you like one more than the other?

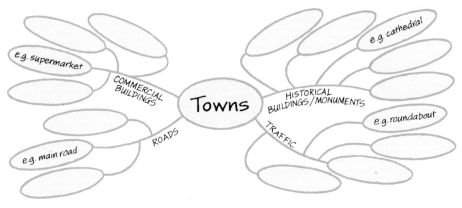

B Now interview your partner about their shoes. Try to ask your questions without looking back at your notes.

REVIEW OF UNIT 3

1 Listen and answer | vocabulary and directions |

Listen to the fifteen questions about the building you are in and write down your answers. Compare your answers with a partner, then check with Tapescript 4 on page 173, and the building.

2 Around town | vocabulary |

Complete the network and then add as many words as possible.

When you have finished, look back at page 18 in Unit 3, to see if you can add any more words.

e.g. supermarket

COMMERCIAL BUILDINGS

e.g. main road

ROADS

Towns

HISTORICAL BUILDINGS/MONUMENTS

e.g. cathedral

e.g. roundabout

TRAFFIC

YOU AND YOUR BODY

Language focus:
adverbs of frequency
reflexive pronouns
giving instructions

Vocabulary:
parts of the body
verbs of movement
time expressions
health and fitness

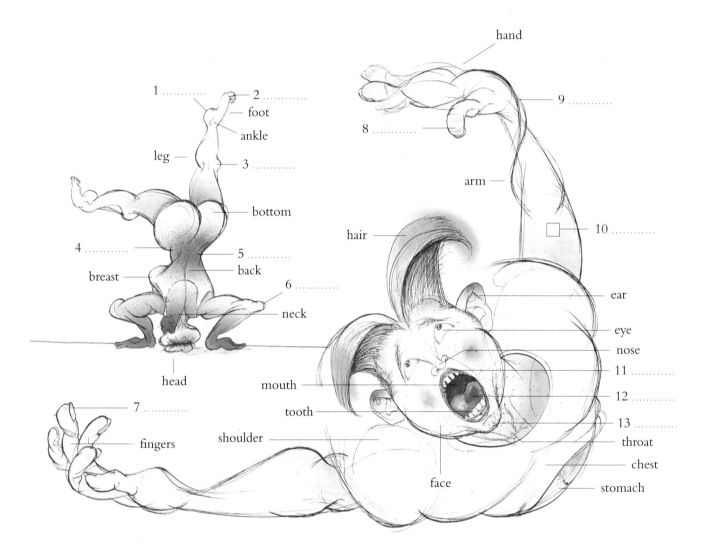

1 Check you know the vocabulary given in the picture, then label the rest using words from the box.

lip	knee	waist	skin	hip	toe	tongue
nail	elbow	wrist	heel	thumb	chin	

Give your book to a partner. Your partner can test you on the new words by pointing to different parts of the body.

2 🎧 Listen to the mathematical quiz on the recording. With a partner, choose your answers from the circle and write them in the boxes.

1. ☐ 5. ☐
2. ☐ 6. ☐
3. ☐ 7. ☐
4. ☐ 8. ☐

3 Look at these things you can do to your body. Work with a partner and underline the wrong answer in each.

1. You can do this to your legs:
   a) hurt them   b) stretch them
   c) break them   d) throw them
2. You can do this to your arms:
   a) bend them   b) shut them
   c) fold them   d) raise them
3. You can do this to your knees:
   a) bend them   b) shake them
   c) cut them   d) scratch them
4. You can do this to your head:
   a) fold it   b) shake it
   c) scratch it   d) hurt it
5. You can do this to your fingers:
   a) bend them   b) shut them
   c) scratch them d) point them
6. You can do this to your eyes:
   a) open them   b) shut them
   c) bend them   d) hurt them

4 Give a partner some instructions, and see if they can follow them.

Example: *Bend your elbows.*
Point your fingers at the board.
Scratch your wrist.

LOOKING AFTER YOURSELF   frequency adverbs; time expressions

1 Organise the time expressions in the box into three groups, using a dictionary if necessary:

1. expressions which tell us when something happened in the past;
2. expressions which tell us how often something happens;
3. expressions which tell us how long something takes.

> half an hour   quite often   hardly ever   twice a year
> whenever I feel like it   every day   the day before yesterday
> a couple of minutes   never   once a week/month/year   every other day
> occasionally   a few days/weeks/months ago   a few seconds

2 Answer these questions using the time expressions. If necessary, say, 'I don't remember'.

    1. Do you ever do the following things? If so, how often?
       do breathing exercises ....
       do yoga ....
       go for a run ....
       ....

    2. How often do you:
       go to the doctor for a check-up? ....
       have an eye test? ....
       weigh yourself? ....
       ....

    3. When did you last:
       feel short of breath after running upstairs? ....
       have a cold? ....
       go to the dentist? ....
       ....

    4. How long do you spend:
       cleaning your teeth? ....
       having a bath or shower? ....
       combing or brushing your hair? ....
       ....

    5. Do you ever do these things? If so, how often?
       take vitamin pills ....
       have a massage ....
       have a sauna or a steam bath ....
       ....

3 Work in small groups. Ask each other the questions and discuss your answers. Remember, if you don't want to answer, you just say:

    I'd rather not say.
or *I'd rather not answer that.*

4 In your groups, think of one more question for each of the five sets of questions above, then move round the class and ask different people your questions.

5 🔲🔲 Most people have an interesting story about a part of their body. Listen to the two speakers on the recording and complete the table.

	Part of body	What happened	Result
Speaker 1	....	....	....
	....	....	....
Speaker 2	....	....	....
	....	....	....

Do you have a story about your own body? Work in small groups. Tell your group about a part of your body, what happened to it and what the result was. (If you haven't got a story, you could tell one about someone you know.)

DIY SURGERY
reflexive pronouns

1 Which word is the 'odd one out' in this group, and why? Work with a partner.

operation   pain   anaesthetic
bandage   recovery   population
surgery   medicine

2 Read the text and answer the question.

What do you do if you are ill and need an operation?

Answer: *you go into hospital, where doctors and nurses look after you and carry out the operation.*

That is true for more than 99.9% of the population, but there are still a few people who believe they can 'do-it-themselves'.

One of the most incredible cases of 'do-it-yourself' surgery is a young man from Wisconsin, USA. He spent months reading books on medicine, and collected all the necessary drugs and instruments. Then one morning, he got up at 4 am and covered his bedroom with clean sheets. He gave himself a light anaesthetic, lay on a table and made a large cut in his chest. He spent most of the day trying to operate on himself, but after eight hours he stopped because of the pain. He managed to bandage himself and call the police, and later he made a full recovery in hospital.

Another strange case was an old man from Eastbourne, who cut off his leg to the knee, although he knew there was nothing wrong with it. His doctor said that he did it to test his willpower and tolerance of pain. When he went to hospital the old man was suffering from shock, but apart from that he was fine.

How do you feel after reading this article?

– the same as you felt before reading it?
– a bit surprised?
– very surprised?
– a bit shocked?
– really shocked?
– absolutely horrified?

Compare your reactions with other members of the group.

3 When you want to show that the subject and object of a verb are the same person, you use a reflexive pronoun.

Examples: *I bandaged* **myself**.   *We introduced* **ourselves**.
Did **you** *cut* **yourself**?   *You can help* **yourselves**.
He burnt **himself** *on the iron.*   *They can look after* **themselves**.

Find the best ending for each of the sentences on the left.

1. I hardly ever look at myself   a. in English.
2. I find it difficult to   b. in the mirror when I get up.
   introduce myself   c. to play a musical instrument.
3. I occasionally cut myself   d. every week.
4. I weigh myself   e. at parties.
5. I often talk to myself   f. without help from other people.
6. I always enjoy myself   g. to strangers.
7. I taught myself   h. when I'm cooking.
8. I can look after myself

In groups, compare your answers, then say if the sentences are true of you.

4 What do you think? Discuss in groups.

- If you are ill, the best place to be is in hospital.
- When it is possible, drugs are better than surgery.
- When you are recovering from an operation, the best thing to do is rest.
- The government should pay for all medical treatment.

PERSONAL STUDY WORKBOOK

In your Personal Study Workbook you will find more exercises to help you with your learning. For Unit 5, these include:

- an exercise on frequency adverbs and time expressions
- more vocabulary exercises
- a reading text about baths
- a listening exercise where you answer questions about yourself
- another page of your visual dictionary – parts of the body

REVIEW AND DEVELOPMENT

REVIEW OF UNIT 3

1 There's a town hall   vocabulary: compounds

Combine words from the left with words from the right to form 14 compound nouns.

Example: *town hall*

town	ring	hall	course
parking	office	store	meter
traffic	pedestrian	lights	road
railway	shopping	office	block
litter	car	stop	crossing
post	department	station	centre
bus	golf	park	bin

2 Word stress in compounds pronunciation

A With most compounds the main stress is on the first word, but sometimes it is on both words.

Examples: First word   Both words
       credit card   common sense
      mother-in-law   mother tongue

Only two of the compound words in the previous exercise have the stress on both words. Which two? Listen and check your answers.

B Give definitions of the compound words from the previous exercise and see if your partner can answer with the correct word and pronunciation.

Example: A: *A place where you can buy a train ticket.*
         B: *A railway station.*

3 Go straight ahead ... directions

A If someone asks you for directions, you can:

1. take them where they want to go.   3. point them in the right general direction.
2. tell them the way.   4. tell them you don't know.

Look at the phrases below and match them with the possibilities above.

a. I'm sorry, I've no idea.   e. I'm afraid I've never heard of it.
b. It's in that direction, but I'm not sure where exactly.   f. I'm going that way – I'll show you.
c. Go along here and ask again.   g. I'm sorry, I'm a stranger here myself.
d. Take the second on the left, and it's right in front of you.   h. Turn left at the traffic lights. It's on your left.

B Think of three places you want to go to in your building or your local area. Then move round the room and ask for directions. When you are giving directions, try to use the phrases above.

REVIEW OF UNIT 4

1 Creative thinking vocabulary

Draw as many objects as possible which include a circle in them.

Examples: *a pair of glasses*   *a tennis ball*

Write the English word next to each one you draw. Use a dictionary if necessary.

2 Interesting experiences present perfect

Look at these examples and then think of three more of your own.

Have you ever   sung a song   in the street?
*   made a speech*

Now ask your questions in groups of three, like this:

A: *Have you ever sung a song in the street?*
B: *Yes, I have.*
A: *Oh, when was that?*
B: *When I went to the carnival last year.*
B: *Have you ever made a speech in the street?*
C: *No, I haven't. Have you?*

6

LEARNING – PAST AND PRESENT

Language focus:	Vocabulary:
present perfect vs. past simple (2)	education
so and *such*	adjectives
spelling rules	
before and *after* + *-ing*	
use of *should*	

AN ADULT LANGUAGE CLASS
education vocabulary; use of should

1 Complete the table on the right using these words:

    lazy   boring
    unpleasant   traditional
    limited   strict   poor
    modern   useless

Type of school:	progressive or ....
Building:	old or ....
Facilities:	good or ....
Books and materials:	useful or ....
Atmosphere:	nice or ....
Teachers:	easy going or ....
Lessons:	interesting or ....
Other learners:	hardworking or ....
Range of subjects:	wide or ....

In groups, use the table to talk about your own secondary school.

Example: *I went to a secondary school that was very traditional, and it was in a big, old building in the centre of the city …*

2 ◻ Listen to a woman talking about her adult language learning class. Is there:

1. anything you think is good about her class?
2. anything you think is bad about her class?

Write down your answers and compare them with a partner.

3 Work in groups and add as many ideas as you can to the table.

An adult class should be …

....

....

....

In an adult class, you should have …

....

....

....

Tell the rest of the class what your group thinks.

4 Look at Tapescript 5 on page 173. With your partner, make a list of useful words and expressions about education, classes and learning.

Examples: *to do a course*   *to be strict*

Now add other words and expressions on the same topic, using a dictionary if necessary.

WAYS OF LEARNING

before and *after* + *-ing*; *so* and *such*; spelling

1 Do you like discovering rules for yourself from examples, or is it better if someone tells you the rule? Tell a partner. Then experiment with the three exercises below.

> **A** Read these sentences. Can you discover a rule for yourself about the use of *before* and *after*?(✓ means correct and ✗ means incorrect)
>
> 1. He left before to say goodbye. (✗)
> 2. I met her after seeing the film. (✓)
> 3. I always clean my teeth before go to bed. (✗)
> 4. After leave the station, she got lost. (✗)
> 5. Before making a decision, think carefully. (✓)
> 6. I often feel ill after to eat ice cream.(✗)
>
> Tell a partner the rule you have discovered.
>
> **B** Here is a spelling rule that is explained to you. Read it and find out when you need to double a consonant and write, for example, *ru__nn__ing* (not *runing*).
>
> In one syllable verbs, if you want to add endings such as *-ing* or *-ed*, you have to double the final consonant when the last three letters are consonant + vowel + consonant.
>
> Examples: c+v+c   plan   pla__nn__ing   pla__nn__ed
>   drop   dro__pp__ing   dro__pp__ed
>
> The exception to this rule are words ending in *y*, *w* or *x*.
>
> Examples: say   saying
>   blow   blowing
>   box   boxed

C *So* and *such* can have the same meaning, but they are used with different constructions. Work with a partner. One of you can read the rule on page 161. The other can discover it for himself/herself from this exercise.

1. The weather was so fantastic that we decided to stay.
2. It was such fantastic weather that we decided to stay.
3. The windows were so big that I couldn't open them.
4. They were such big windows that I couldn't open them.
5. He was so slow that he didn't finish the exercise.
6. He was such a slow worker that he didn't finish the exercise.

If you discovered the rule for yourself, explain it to your partner. If you read the rule on page 161, think of two sentences which show the rule.

2 Work with a partner. See if you have understood the rules, using these exercises.

Write sentences using *so* or *such*:

Write sentences using *before* or *after*:

Complete these verbs and double the consonant where necessary.

Examples: *help* + *ed* = **helped**
           swim + *ing* = **swimming**

stop + ed =	start + ing =	win + ing =	meet + ing =
look + ed =	rob + ed =	cry + ing =	climb + ed =

3 In groups, discuss these questions.

- Are there rules we need to discover for ourselves?
- Are there rules that other people should explain to us?
- Are there rules we need to read?
- Which takes more time: discovering rules, or reading/hearing about them?
- Which do you feel helps you to remember the rule for a longer time?
- Do you think adults and children have different preferences?

1 Read the phrases in the table below. Check any new words in your dictionary.

	You	Most people	Your ideal age
learn to use a computer			
learn to speak a foreign language			
learn to look after children			
learn to look after your own money			
learn to drive a car			
learn to manage stress			
learn to look after old people			
learn to listen to other people			
learn to swim			
learn to work effectively			

How many of these things can you do, and at what age did you learn to do them?

When do most people learn to do them?

What's the ideal age to learn them?

Complete the table above, and then discuss your answers in groups.

2 Here are some things which happen in class. Read the list and ask your teacher or partner if you don't understand them.

You …
– speak to the person next to you.
– look things up in a dictionary.
– learn new words.
– study some new grammar.
– read something in English.
– do exercises.
– make mistakes.
– express your opinion.
– answer questions.
– use your own language.
– write things in your notebook.
– laugh at things.
– ask the teacher a question.

3 Now think about your lesson so far today. Make sentences about what you have done, and what you haven't done, using the present perfect tense (*have* + past participle) and the list in Exercise 2:

Example: *So far in this lesson …*
    – I've learnt four new words.
    – I've used my dictionary three times.
    – I haven't asked the teacher anything.
    – I've written lots of things in my notebook.

Tell your partner.

4 Now think about the last lesson you had. Make sentences with your partner, using the past simple.

Examples: *In the last lesson, I didn't understand everything, but Marta did.*
    In the last lesson, we spoke to each other a lot.

5 In Exercise 3, you used the present perfect. In Exercise 4 you used the past simple.

Now, either

1. Look at the two exercises and try to decide when we use one tense and when we use the other. Compare your answers with a partner.

or

2. Use the Grammar Reference on page 161 to find out.

6 Think of three things you have done so far this week or this month that you didn't do last week or last month. Tell a partner.

Examples: *I've used my computer a lot this week, but I didn't use it at all last week.*
I've played tennis twice this week, but I didn't play last week.

PERSONAL STUDY WORKBOOK

In your Personal Study Workbook, you will find more exercises to help you with your learning. For Unit 6, these include:

- an exercise on the present perfect and past simple and one on *so* and *such*
- a vocabulary exercise to help you use a dictionary
- another listen and answer activity
- a text about juggling and a poem to read
- more spelling rules and a spelling test

REVIEW AND DEVELOPMENT

REVIEW OF UNIT 4

1 What are you doing here?   vocabulary

Read the dialogue and answer the questions below.

(Rob arrives at Jean and Dave's house.)

JEAN: Rob!
ROB: *(with a big smile)* Hello, Jean.
JEAN: Well, come in – what a lovely surprise!
It's completely mad here today – it's the children's birthday party and I have to go to the baker's …
DAVE: Rob! How marvellous to see you!
What are you doing here?
ROB: Hi, Dave, er, well, um, look, don't you remember – you invited me for lunch today.
DAVE: Oh, dear, yes, you're right – Jean, I'm terribly sorry – I completely forgot.
ROB: Look, why don't I come another day?
JEAN: No, Rob, stay for the party.
ROB: No, it's all right, don't worry. Perhaps I could come next week instead.
JEAN: No! Rob! Come back!
(angrily) Oh really, Dave, you are hopeless!

1. Does Dave greet Rob before or after Jean does?
2. Does Rob apologise to anyone?
3. Who is in a bit of a panic?
4. Who is pleased to see who?
5. Who is embarrassed?
6. Who makes a suggestion?
7. Who refuses to do something?
8. Does Dave apologise to Jean?
9. Does Jean get angry with anyone?

Work in groups of three. Practise the dialogue until you can do it without looking. Try to show how each person feels.

2 Have you ever ...? | present perfect |

Move round the class asking the following questions. If you get a positive answer, find out more information by asking another question.

Have you ever:
– broken your leg?
– done yoga?
– had an operation?
– looked after an animal for someone?
– killed an animal?
– given blood?
– seen a road accident?

Tell other members of the class something interesting that you have discovered.

Examples: *Pierre has given blood ten times.*
Mario broke his leg skiing last year.

REVIEW OF UNIT 5

1 Listen and answer | vocabulary |

A ⊂⊃ Think of a person standing up. Now listen to the recording and write down your answers.

You will find the questions in Tapescript 6 on page 174. Check your answers.

B Tell your partner to close the book and read the questions quickly. See if they can answer correctly.

2 I burnt myself | vocabulary; reflexive pronouns |

Complete the sentences with verbs from the left and pronouns from the right. If necessary look at the irregular verbs list on page 175.

Verbs	*Pronouns*
burn	myself
introduce	himself
look after	ourselves
help	themselves
look at	yourself
hurt	herself
weigh	yourselves
cut	

1. She .... when she lit the fire.
2. The children .... when we went out.
3. I'm afraid I .... using that knife.
4. We .... to the host.
5. Did you .... when you fell off that chair?
6. He was quite shocked when he .... in the mirror.
7. I .... using the scales in the bathroom.
8. Nobody was there to serve the food so we ....

LETTERS THAT TELL A STORY

Language focus:
comparative and superlative adjectives
(don't) have to / need to
spelling

Vocabulary:
types of text
describing personality/character
professions
word building
synonyms and opposites

---

1 🔲 Listen to the recording and write down what you hear.

2 What have you just written?
The answer is one of the following:

an essay	a formal letter	an addressed envelope
a recipe	a job application	a telephone message
a diary entry	an informal letter	an immigration form

3 Now match these examples with the words above.

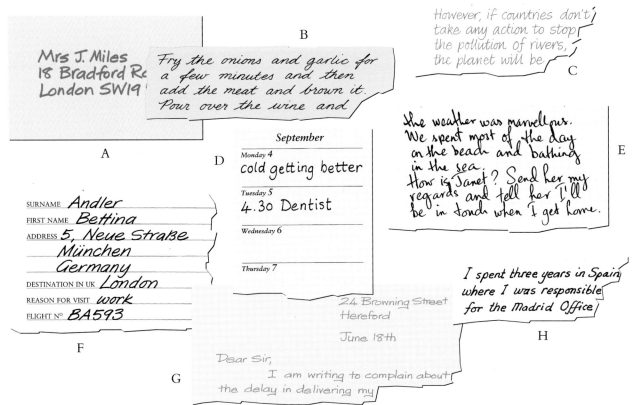

Think back carefully over the last 2–3 months. How many of the above have you
written/completed? Compare your answers in groups. Who has written the most, and why?

Example: *I haven't written any essays, but I've addressed lots of envelopes*
because I moved house last month and I had to write and tell everyone.

---

4 Look carefully at the handwriting in Exercise 3 and complete these sentences. More than one answer may be possible.

1. A's handwriting is bigger than ....
2. D's handwriting is easier to read than ....
3. B's handwriting is more attractive than ....
4. C's handwriting is neater than ....
5. G's handwriting is more adult than ....
6. F's handwriting is more uniform than ....

Read your sentences in groups and discuss them.

5 Now answer these questions.

1. Whose handwriting is the biggest?
2. Whose handwriting is the easiest to read?
3. Whose handwriting is the most attractive?
4. Whose handwriting is the neatest?
5. Whose handwriting is the most childish?
6. Whose handwriting is the most uniform?
7. Whose handwriting is the best?
8. Whose handwriting is the worst?

Compare your answers in groups.

6 Write answers to the following questions. Compare your answers with a partner, and then check in the Grammar Reference on page 162.

1. What are the two different forms used to make comparative adjectives in English? What is the rule for the use of each one?
2. What are the two different forms used to make superlative adjectives in English? What is the rule for the use of each one?

7 Work in small groups. Look at the dictations you wrote at the beginning of the lesson, and compare your different handwriting using comparatives and superlatives.

WHAT YOUR WRITING REVEALS
vocabulary: wordbuilding; (don't) have to / need to

1 Complete the table and check that you understand and can say the words.
Use a dictionary and your teacher to help you.

Adjective	Noun
....	reliability
....	honesty
....	imagination
....	popularity
....	sensitivity
....	self-confidence
....	art
....	intelligence

2 Which of these characteristics do you need for the jobs in the box? Choose some and discuss your answers in groups, using the expressions below.

lawyer	architect
personnel manager	comedian
vet	plumber
accountant	politician
English teacher	surgeon

A (lawyer) needs to be (honest). has to be ...

A (plumber) doesn't have to be ... need to be ...

It helps if a (politician) is ...

3 How can an employer find an applicant for a job with the necessary characteristics? Here is one solution. Read the text, and answer the questions.

What your writing reveals

IN A GARDEN room at the back of her house, Renna Nezos sits at her desk. In front of her is a large sheet of yellow paper. She looks carefully at the small writing squeezed uncomfortably into one corner of the page. There is definitely something strange about it.

Mrs Nezos holds the paper up to the light and speaks rapidly into the telephone. 'There is a tremor in the writing. I think there could be several explanations. Epilepsy. Alcohol perhaps. Or even drugs...' There is a silence as the listener – a personnel manager at S G Warburg – digests this unexpected news.

Mrs Nezos is principal of the London Academy of Graphology and is a professional graphologist who has analysed 25,000 samples of handwriting over the past 20 years. It is her job to examine the handwriting she is sent for hidden characteristics and possible weaknesses.

And she is not alone. In Europe, graphology is popular in business. Swiss companies use it in at least 50% of general management appointments, while in France and Germany it is even more common than that.

Mrs Nezos does not say she can guess the age or gender of the writer, stupidity, looks or destiny. But she believes that handwriting can show if someone is sensitive, imaginative, reliable or honest.

True or false? Compare with a partner.

1. Mrs Nezos looks at people's handwriting and believes she can tell something of their character.
2. She is very experienced.
3. She can tell the sex of the writer, and how old they are.
4. At the moment she is analysing the handwriting of the personnel manager at S G Warburg.
5. Graphology (reading character in handwriting) is used quite often to help select employees for jobs in Europe.

4 Discuss in groups.

1. Do you believe her?
2. Do you think it is a good idea for companies to use handwriting analysis in job applications?
3. If companies use handwriting analysis, should they tell the candidates?
4. Do you think handwriting analysis is more useful for some jobs than others?

1 Have you ever opened another person's letter by mistake or because you wanted to read it? If so, why and what happened? Discuss in small groups.

2 Work with a partner. Can you find pairs of words in the circle that are connected in some way?

Examples: *To lie* and *to tell the truth* are opposites.
If someone disappears, you try to find them.
Upset means sad and angry.

mail   brave

wicked   necklace

real   nonsense   to lie

to disappear   a trick   post

sad and angry   evil

handkerchief   nose   magician

to tell the truth   find

imaginary   courage

rubbish   upset

jewels

Compare your connections with those of another pair.

3 🔊 You are going to listen to a story by Saki called *Shock Tactics*. Look at the people in the picture and then read the letters. Who wrote the letters, and can you imagine why? Tell your partner, then listen to the recording.

| *Ella McCarthy,* | *Bertie Heasant* | *Mrs Heasant,* | *Clovis Sangrail,* |
| *a friend of Bertie's* | | *Bertie's mother* | *a friend of Bertie's* |

My dearest Bertie,
Do you think you will be brave enough to do it? It will take some courage. Don't forget the jewels. They are a detail, but details interest me.
Yours as ever,
Clothilde
Your mother must not know of my existence. If she asks you about me, tell her you have never heard of me.

So you have really done it. Poor girl! Poor Dagmar! Now she is finished, I almost feel sorry for her. You did it very well, you wicked boy; the servants all think she killed herself, and there will be no trouble. But it will be best not to touch the jewels just yet.
Clothilde

Dear Bertie,
I hope you aren't upset about the stupid letters that I have been sending in the name of an imaginary Clothilde. You told me the other day that the servants, or somebody at your home, opened your letters, so I thought I would give anyone that opened them something exciting to read. The shock may do them good.
Yours,
Clovis Sangrail

4 Work with your partner and complete these sentences. Then discuss your reactions to the story.

1. Bertie gave Ella some .... as a present.
2. She couldn't write to .... because Bertie's mother ....
3. Bertie told .... about the problem.
4. Clovis .... two letters to Bertie and signed them ....
5. Mrs Heasant opened .... two letters and was very ....
6. Bertie said ....
7. When she read the last letter, she ....
8. She promised ....

5 This is the letter Ella wanted to write. Unfortunately, she had some problems with spelling (8) and punctuation (4) and capital letters (2). Correct her mistakes with your partner.

16 Kensington Gardens, London W8

14th march 1913

Dear Bertie!

I'm just writting to thank you for the wonderfull handkerchiefs that I recieved in this morning's male, you always find the prettyest gifts and you know how much I adore beatiful things.

I sincerly hope you will come and visite me soon and then I can thank you in person.

With best wishes,

Ella

6 With your partner, write a short 'thank you' letter to another pair for an imaginary present.

PERSONAL STUDY WORKBOOK

In your Personal Study Workbook, you will find more exercises to help you with your learning. For Unit 7, these include:

- an exercise to practise comparatives
- vocabulary exercises on word building and collocation
- listening to people talking about how they learnt to write
- an opportunity to analyse your handwriting through a reading text
- writing exercises on spelling and letter writing

REVIEW AND DEVELOPMENT

REVIEW OF UNIT 5

1 Parts of the body | vocabulary |

Answer these questions, then compare with a partner.

1. Which is heavier: your head, or your leg and foot together?
2. Which is nearer to your lips: your eyes or your ears?
3. Which is bigger: the diameter of your wrist, or the diameter of your ankle?
4. Which is longer: the distance from your wrist to your elbow, or the length of your foot?
5. Which is greater: the number of teeth you have, or the number of fingers and toes together?
6. Which is bigger: your thumbnail or your little toenail?
7. Which is smaller: the diameter of your waist or the diameter of your chest?
8. Which is smaller: the palm of your hand or your knee?

2 How to pronounce the letters 'th' | pronunciation |

The letters 'th' have two different pronunciations. Listen to the recording.

Examples: *this; then; mother* /ð/
think; fourth; mouth /θ/

Put the words into the correct column, then check your answers on the recording.

bath, there, breath, breathe, teeth, thumb, another, throat, themselves, without	Column 1 /θ/	Column 2 /ð/
	....	....
	....	....
	....	....
	....	....
	....	....

Practise saying the words with your partner.

3 Did you teach yourself? | reflexive pronouns |

Look at the table below. Can you do these things? Did you teach yourself or did someone else teach you? Put ticks (✓) in the correct columns.

	Yes	No	Taught myself	Someone else taught me
1. swim	......	......	......	......
2. play poker	......	......	......	......
3. use a camcorder	......	......	......	......
4. ride a bike	......	......	......	......
5. sew	......	......	......	......
6. cook	......	......	......	......
7. iron	......	......	......	......
8. type	......	......	......	......

Write three more things you taught yourself to do. Then compare your information in small groups.

REVIEW OF UNIT 6

1 Listen and answer | past simple and present perfect |

CD Listen to the recording and write down your answers. Compare your answers with a partner and then check with Tapescript 7 on page 174. Tell your partner to close their book, then read the questions quickly to them. Can they answer correctly?

2 Present and past participles | spelling |

A Write down the present participles of these verbs and then check your answers with a partner.

Examples: *sit/sitting*　*fight/fighting*

put	meet	feel	set	come
plan	sail	drop	start	climb
rob	hit	bite	clean	win
write	say	swim	use	stop

B Now write the past participles. Some are irregular, some are regular. Then compare with a partner.

3 There was such a lot of traffic | so and such |

Think of an explanation for each of the questions below, using *so* or *such*. Work with a partner.

Example: *Why were you late for the meeting?*
　　　　Because there was such a lot of traffic.

1. Why didn't you telephone me last night?
2. Why did you miss the plane?
3. Why did you leave the party early?
4. Why haven't you finished this report?
5. Why haven't you done these exercises?
6. Why did you take a taxi?

Find a new partner and practise the questions and answers.

8

TAKE IT OR LEAVE IT

Language focus:	Vocabulary:
going to and *might* for future plans	shopping expressions
present continuous for future arrangements	phrasal verbs
will for spontaneous decisions	services, e.g. public transport, insurance

BUYING SOMETHING TO WEAR
phrasal verbs; shopping expressions; will

1 Read through the statements and put them in the correct order. Compare your answers with a partner.

You show the assistant your receipt.
You get a receipt.
1 You look for the item of clothing you want.
You take it off and try another one on.
You decide to buy it.
You take it home and discover a problem with it.
You try it on.
You get your money back.
You pay for it.
You take it back.
You ask for a refund.

2 Match these sentences with the statements in Exercise 1. Compare your answers with a partner.

Example: *Here's my receipt.* = *You show the assistant your receipt.*

Here's my receipt.
Excuse me, where's the changing room?
I'll take it.
Do you take American Express?
Oh, no, there's something wrong with it.
Excuse me, I'm looking for a sweater.
Could I have my money back, please?
I'm afraid it doesn't fit.
Here's your receipt.
I bought this here last week and I'm afraid …
Thank you.

3 Work with a partner. Write a shopping dialogue using the sentences above. You will need to decide what you are buying and what is wrong with it, and invent most of the shop assistant's part. Then practise your dialogue.

4 When the person decided to buy the sweater in the shopping dialogue, she said, 'I'll take it.'

We use *will* in this situation when we are making a decision at the moment of speaking. Here is another example:

(*Doorbell rings*)
JACK: Mary! I'm in the kitchen!
MARY: OK. I'll answer it.

Now work with a partner and think of spontaneous answers to these sentences:

Example: *It's cold in this room.*
　　　　　Answer: *OK, I'll turn on the heater.*
　　　　　or　　　*OK, I'll close the window.*

1. It's hot in this room.
2. These plates are dirty.
3. The phone's ringing.
4. It's very dark in here.
5. We haven't got any coffee.
6. I can't hear the radio.

5 📼 Listen to the recording and shout spontaneous answers.

1 What kind of shops are these? Identify them with a partner.

2 Do you have any shopping plans over the next few days? Complete the table below.

(✓) = I'm going to buy something.

(?) = I might buy something.

(✗) = I'm definitely not going to buy anything.

	Yes or no? ✓ ? ✗	What?
a jeweller's	✓	earrings for my sister's birthday
a supermarket		
a street market		
a department store		
a chemist's		
an electrical shop		
a clothes shop		
a greengrocer's		
(anywhere else you like)		

Now tell your partner your plans using the structures in the box, like this:

A: Are you going shopping this week?

B: Yes, I'm going to buy a few things at the supermarket.

A: Oh, what?

B: Food for the weekend. And I might buy something from a clothes shop this week.

A: What?

B: Trousers, if I can find a pair that I like.

3 Do the following quiz with a partner. There is only one correct answer for each question.

Ways of talking about the future

① A friend is planning to buy a compact disc player at the weekend. What does she tell you?

a. I buy a CD player this weekend.

b. I'll buy a CD player this weekend.

c. I'm going to buy a CD player this weekend.

② She wants someone to go with her to give her some advice. You are free at the weekend. What do you say?

a. OK, I come with you.

b. OK, I'll come with you.

c. OK, I'm going to come with you.

③ It is now the weekend. You are leaving the house. What do you shout to someone in the house, as you shut the door?

a. I go to meet Susan. See you later.

b. I'll go to meet Susan. See you later.

c. I'm going to meet Susan. See you later.

④ Your friend's mother has agreed to lend her the money for this expensive item. So when you ask her how she is going to pay for it, what does she answer?

a. I borrow the money from my mother.

b. I'll borrow the money from my mother.

c. I'm borrowing the money from my mother.

⑤ Your friend looks at several CD players, but she cannot choose between any of them. You get impatient and tell her she must make a decision, so finally she says:

a. No – I leave it.

b. No – I'll leave it.

c. No – I'm leaving it.

⑥ You leave the shop together. You invite your friend for a meal this evening. What does she answer?

a. I'd love to, but my sister is coming over to see me.

b. I'd love to, but my sister will come over to see me.

c. I'd love to, but my sister comes over to see me.

Check the answers with your teacher.

4 Complete these rules, using the words in the box.

> the present continuous   going to (do)   will

---

1. We use .... to talk about plans and intentions, when we have decided in the past about an action in the future.

Example: I .... (work) hard next year.
(I thought about it in the past and made a decision before now.)

2. We use .... when we decide something at the moment of speaking, not before.

Example: a: Would you like a drink?
b: Yes, please, I .... (have) a coffee.

3. We use .... to talk about plans and arrangements we have made in advance with other people.

Example: I .... (have) lunch with Jenny tomorrow.
(I phoned her yesterday and we made the arrangements.)

Compare with a partner then check your answers in the Grammar Reference on pages 162 and 163.

1 Look at the list below and check that you understand the words. How do you pay for these? Talk to your partner. Then add two more things to the list and ask your partner about them.

Examples: *I pay for supermarket shopping in cash.*
                               by cheque.
                               by credit card.

              I pay my electricity bill by debit card.
                               by direct debit.

	American speaker	British speaker
supermarket shopping		
petrol for your car		
new clothes		
daily/weekly transport		
an airline ticket		
car insurance		
stamps		
a restaurant meal		
a phone bill		
(other)		

2 ⬚ The speakers on the recording are from America and Britain. How do they pay for these things? Complete the table in Exercise 1.

Compare your answers with your partner. Do any answers surprise you?

3 Work in small groups and check you understand the words in the list on the right. In your country, are these things free, cheap or expensive?

soap ....

local phone calls ....

health care ....

public transport ....

rice ....

art galleries ....

tobacco ....

libraries ....

tap water ....

car alarms ....

textbooks for schoolchildren ....

heating/air conditioning ....

4 In your groups, can you think of one good reason in each case why these things should be free for everyone?

When you have all finished, tell the class.

PERSONAL STUDY WORKBOOK

In your Personal Study Workbook, you will find more exercises to help you with your learning. For Unit 8, these include:

- exercises on ways of expressing the future
- two vocabulary exercises, including idiomatic expressions
- an exercise to test your understanding of pronunciation
- texts to read about cosmopolitan shops in London
- listening and writing activities
- another page of your visual dictionary – clothes, phrasal verbs

---

REVIEW AND DEVELOPMENT

REVIEW OF UNIT 6

1 What was your school like? | vocabulary |

Transform this text to give the opposite of each word underlined.

My secondary school was very ~~traditional~~ *progressive* and was in a big, old building, but it had very good facilities and it offered a wide range of subjects to study. The books our teachers used were useless and the lessons were generally quite boring. The atmosphere was very unpleasant, partly because the teachers were strict, but perhaps too because most of the students were lazy.

2 Do this exercise | vocabulary: *do* or *make?* |

Do you use *do* or *make* with these nouns?

an exercise   a noise   friends   an exam   a mistake
a mess   a course   one's best   homework   progress

With a partner write a paragraph (maximum 100 words) about your English class and see how many of the above phrases you can include. When you have finished, read your paragraph to another pair.

REVIEW OF UNIT 7

1 A spelling test | dictation/spelling |

CD Listen and write down the sentences you hear. At the end, check with a partner and then look at Tapescript 8 on page 174 for the correct spelling.

2 Who has the longest hair? | superlatives |

Do you know the answers to these questions? Write down what you think is the correct answer. Guess if you don't know.

1. Who has the longest hair in your class?
2. Who is wearing the smallest pair of shoes?
3. Who has the most difficult job in the class?
4. Who has the smallest handwriting?
5. Who is the youngest in the class?
6. Who speaks the most languages?
7. Who makes the fewest mistakes in English?
8. Who has the shortest journey to school?
9. Who has the largest number of brothers and sisters?
10. Who wears the most unusual clothes?

Now move around the class and ask questions to find out if you were right.

3 A changing world | speaking |

In our modern world there are many things that are always written on a typewriter or computer. But there are still some things that are handwritten. Add to the table and compare your answers in groups.

Usually typed	Usually handwritten	Both
a company report	a shopping list	an essay

9

FOOD AND DRINK

Language focus:	Vocabulary:
present simple passive	what to say in restaurants
have to, don't have to	food and drink
must, mustn't	
should, shouldn't	

DRINKS AROUND THE WORLD

1 Here are some drinks. Which ones have you drunk recently and why? Tell a partner.

a glass of water   a glass of milk
a cup of tea   a glass of champagne
a cola   a liqueur

2 What do you know about drinks around the world? In small groups look at these statements and tick the correct columns.

	True	False	Don't know
1. Kenya is the largest producer of coffee in the world.	......	......	......
2. In Morocco, tea is usually served in small glasses.	......	......	......
3. Japanese rice wine (*sake*) is usually served hot.	......	......	......
4. Turkish coffee is made by boiling water, sugar and coffee together.	......	......	......
5. In Britain, tea is usually drunk with lemon.	......	......	......
6. A real bottle of Mezcal from Mexico should have a worm in it.	......	......	......
7. Cola is made from a small, black fruit that is grown in North America.	......	......	......
8. In Sweden, people often drink milk with meatballs.	......	......	......
9. You should store wine horizontally.	......	......	......
10. Irish coffee contains Irish whiskey, beer and fresh cream.	......	......	......

Check your answers with your teacher. If there are any mistakes in the sentences, write in the corrections.

3 Look at these sentences:

In Morocco, tea is served in small glasses.
Tea is drunk with lemon.
Cola is made from a small black fruit.

These are examples of the present simple passive: the verb *to be* + past participle. We use this because we are more interested here in *what is done* than who does it.

Complete these sentences with a partner in a suitable way.

Coffee is produced ....
Cola is sold ....
Cognac is sometimes drunk ....
.... is grown ....
.... is made from ....
.... is drunk ....
.... is exported ....
Champagne ....
Tea ....
Mineral water ....

Move around the class and compare your sentences.

FOOD AND DRINK: DOS AND DON'TS   *have to, don't have to, must(n't) and should(n't)*

1 Match these sentence halves.

You have to/must	eat seafood which isn't fresh.
You should	wash melon before you eat it.
You don't have to	go on a diet if you are overweight.
You shouldn't	pay for a meal in a restaurant.
You mustn't	eat apples which aren't ripe.

Compare your answers with a partner, then match
these explanations with the example sentences.

1. It is a good idea to do it.
2. It isn't a good idea to do it.
3. You can do it if you want, but it's not necessary.
4. It is necessary or an obligation to do this.
5. It is wrong or dangerous, or sometimes not permitted.

2 Work with a partner. Study the sentences and decide if they are true or not. If they aren't true, correct them.

Example: *You have to put lemon in tea or coffee.*
Answer: *Not true. You don't have to put anything in tea or coffee, but you can if you want.*

1. You don't have to keep garlic in the fridge.
2. You have to drink wine if you are taking medicine.
3. You shouldn't cook potatoes before eating them.
4. You should always cook carrots.
5. You mustn't eat potatoes if they are green.
6. You don't have to wash lettuce before eating it.
7. You mustn't peel peaches before eating them.
8. You don't have to keep yoghurt in a cool place.

3 Dorinda visits some English friends for dinner. Read what happens.

They invite Dorinda for dinner at 8.00, and she arrives at 7.30. At the door, she takes off her shoes and gives them some ice cream for the dessert, and a bottle of wine. They offer her a drink, which she politely refuses. Five minutes later, she pours herself a glass of wine.

At the table, they serve the onion soup, first to Dorinda, who starts eating immediately. She breaks her bread into the soup, and when she has finished she helps herself to some more. She then has a cigarette while she waits for everyone else to finish. The next course is beef, which she refuses without giving a reason. She is offered some chicken, which she eats, mostly with her fingers. She finishes her meal, leaving her knife and fork on the table.

During the meal, she talks very little and doesn't say anything about the food. She also refuses dessert, saying she is on a diet. After dinner, she stays for about 15 minutes, then says, 'I really have to go now,' and leaves immediately.

The next day, she telephones, saying how much she enjoyed the evening, and asks for the recipe for the soup.

4 Which of Dorinda's actions are acceptable in your country, and which are not? Discuss in groups.

You should ....
You shouldn't ....
You mustn't ....
You don't have to ....
If you ...., you should ....
In my country, people usually ....
In my country, people don't usually ....
It's (a bit) rude to ....

1 Work with a partner and choose the correct answer to these questions. Sometimes more than one answer is correct.

1. You arrive at a restaurant with two friends but you haven't booked a table. The waitress welcomes you. What do you say?
   a. Have you any seats left?
   b. Have you got a table for three?
   c. I want a table for three.

2. You sit down and call the waitress. What do you say?
   a. Waitress!
   b. Excuse me!
   c. Hey!

3. What is your next question?
   a. Bring me the menu.
   b. Could we see the menu, please?
   c. Could we see the card, please?

4. You and your friends have decided what you want to eat. The waitress says, 'Are you ready to order?' You are. What do you say?
   a. I'd like bean soup to start with.
   b. I think I'll have bean soup.
   c. I take bean soup.

5. When you begin the main course, you find there are certain things you need. Which of these can you say?
   a. Excuse me, I haven't got a fork.
   b. I need salt.
   c. Could you bring me some more bread, please?

6. You want to wash your hands. What do you ask?
   a. Excuse me, where are the services?
   b. Excuse me, where is the toilet?
   c. Excuse me, where is the washroom?

7. After the dessert and coffee, you want to pay for the meal. What do you say to the waitress?
   a. Could you give me the account, please?
   b. Could I have the bill, please?
   c. Could you bring me the check, please?

2 📼 Listen to the recording and mark the answers you hear. Compare with a partner.

3 Look at the menu. Do these things appear in your country (often/occasionally/never)?

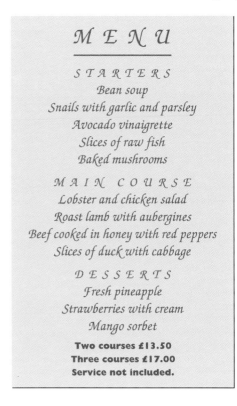

M E N U
────────────
S T A R T E R S
Bean soup
Snails with garlic and parsley
Avocado vinaigrette
Slices of raw fish
Baked mushrooms

M A I N   C O U R S E
Lobster and chicken salad
Roast lamb with aubergines
Beef cooked in honey with red peppers
Slices of duck with cabbage

D E S S E R T S
Fresh pineapple
Strawberries with cream
Mango sorbet

Two courses £13.50
Three courses £17.00
Service not included.

4 Work in groups of four. Three of you are going to the restaurant above, the fourth person is the waiter/waitress. Practise the different parts of the evening meal, in English.

PERSONAL STUDY WORKBOOK

In your Personal Study Workbook, you will find more exercises to help you with your learning. For Unit 9, these include:

- an exercise to practise *must*, *have to* and *should*, and another to practise the present simple passive
- a vocabulary activity about restaurants, and another to revise food
- listening to restaurant conversations
- reading about drinks around the world
- sequencing ideas in writing
- the next page of your visual dictionary – food

REVIEW AND DEVELOPMENT

REVIEW OF UNIT 7

1 Syllables and word stress   pronunciation

A You need to know the number of syllables in a word to pronounce it correctly.

Examples: *broken: bro-ken* (2 syllables)
cinema: cin-e-ma (3 syllables)
education: ed-u-ca-tion (4 syllables)

How many syllables are there in each of these words?

message	diary	punctuation	thousand
cheque	envelope	reliability	recipe

B ☐☐ Which syllable in these words has the main stress? Put them in the correct columns below. Listen and check your answers, then practise saying the words with a partner.

politics	intelligent	sensitivity	reliable	politician
architect	imaginative	popularity	necessary	
advertising	advertisement	analysis	sensitive	
personnel	character	computer	application	

1st syllable	*2nd syllable*	*3rd syllable*
politics	intelligent	sensitivity

2 Word partnerships vocabulary: collocation

Writing is just one of the things you do by hand. Look at the list below and decide if:

- you can do it with one hand easily.
- you can do it with one hand but with difficulty.
- you need two hands.

1. make a phone call
2. ride a bike
3. drive a car
4. play a flute
5. use a word processor

6. wrap up a birthday present
7. pack a suitcase
8. eat a pizza
9. lock a door
10. take a photo

REVIEW OF UNIT 8

1 Future plans and arrangements going to + infinitive, might; present continuous

Complete the table about yourself.

Definite plans and intentions	Possible plans	Arrangements
This week I'm going to	I might	I'm ....ing ....
This year I'm going to	I might	I'm ....ing ....

Find out about other people's plans and arrangements.

2 Shopping round the world speaking

Discuss these questions in small groups.

In your country:
- If you take something back to a shop, is it easy to get a refund?
- If you take something back, does the assistant usually ask you for a receipt?
- Do you need to show a cheque guarantee card if you write a cheque?
- Are shop assistants usually rude or polite?
- Do all clothes shops have changing rooms? If so, what are they like?
- What can you buy in a chemist's, apart from medicine?
- Are department stores common in your country?
- Do any shops have their own credit cards?

FEELINGS:
THE GOOD, THE BAD AND THE UGLY

> Language focus:
> verbs with *-ing* form or infinitive
> *could* for suggestions
> expressing feelings: *it makes me …*
> *I get … when …*
>
> Vocabulary:
> emotions
> verb + noun collocations

1 How do you feel about the following?
Talk to two other people.

- writing letters to friends and family
- writing official or business letters
- receiving letters from friends and family
- receiving letters from companies selling things
  ('junk mail')
- getting phone calls after ten o'clock at night
- people visiting you unexpectedly
- meeting new people
- strangers talking to you on buses and trains

2 Work with a partner and match the sentences with the pictures.

a. I <u>hate</u> wearing suits.
b. I quite <u>enjoy</u> going to the dentist.
c. I <u>want</u> to be a millionaire by the time I'm 50.
d. I <u>don't mind</u> getting up early.
e. I <u>can't stand</u> doing housework.
f. I <u>regret</u> getting married.
g. I <u>would like</u> to die peacefully in bed.
h. I <u>love</u> repairing things.

Move around the class. Find at least one person who agrees with each of the sentences.

3 How are *want* and *would like* different from the other underlined verbs in Exercise 2?

A good dictionary will tell you if a verb is followed by a special construction e.g. an infinitive or an *-ing* form:

en·joy *(obj)* [PLEASURE] /ɪnˈdʒɔɪ/ *v* to get pleasure from (something) ● *I really enjoyed that film/book/concert/party/meal.* [T] ● *I was really surprised that I enjoyed the exams!* [T] ● *I want to travel because I enjoy meeting people and seeing new places.* [+ v-ing]

(from the *Cambridge International Dictionary of English*)

enjoy /ɪ'ndʒɔɪ/, **enjoys, enjoying, enjoyed.** 1 If you **enjoy** something, 1.1 you find pleasure and satisfaction in doing or experiencing it. ᴇɢ *I enjoyed the holiday enormously... She is someone who loves people and enjoys life... Painting is something that I really enjoy doing.*   v+o, OR v+-ing
= like
≠ dislike

(from *Collins COBUILD English Language Dictionary*)

en·joy /ɪnˈdʒɔɪ/ *v* **-joyed, -joying** [T] **1** [+ *v-ing*] to get happiness from; like: *I enjoyed the film/I always enjoy going to the cinema.*

(from *Longman Active Study Dictionary of English*)

4 Are these verbs followed by an infinitive or an *-ing* form? Use a dictionary to check your answers and look up the meaning, if necessary.

refuse   expect   give up   decide   imagine
avoid   hope   finish   promise   offer

5 Complete these sentences about yourself.

1. I hope .... next year.
2. I can't stand .... in class.
3. I decided .... last year.
4. I always avoid .... if possible.
5. I want .... at some time in the future.
6. I'd like .... during this course.
7. I can't imagine .... country.
8. I'd like to give up ....,... as soon as possible.

Compare your answers in groups.

1 Read the poem and underline the words which describe the pictures.

Asked what makes her happy, nursing sister
   Georgina Salmon listed:
Log fires and Christmas tree lights
Being alone; walking the dog in the country,
   surrounded by fields
Jacket potatoes oozing with butter
Receiving long letters from friends not often seen
Newborn babies and the expressions they make
A mother's expression when she sees her baby for the
   first time
Books and music
The car starting first time in winter

The look on children's faces as you tell them a story
Knowing a patient will recover when at times it's
   seemed impossible
Bubble baths and the feeling after a sauna
Looking at my old photographs
Watching a good suspense film
Church bells
Taking communion and knowing that God is real
Liqueur coffee after a delicious meal
Robins watching you as you dig over the garden
Waking up to the knowledge that it's a day off from
   work.

▭▭ Now listen to the poem and follow in your book.

2 With a partner, answer these questions about Georgina Salmon.

Example: *Is she married?* *We don't know but probably not, because she doesn't talk about a husband.*
Can she drive? *Yes, because she talks about the car starting in winter.*

1. Has she got any children?
2. Has she got any pets?
3. Is she religious?
4. Has she got any outdoor hobbies?
5. Does she drink?

6. Does she live in a hot country?
7. Does she find her job rewarding?
8. Does she enjoy her spare time?
9. Is she optimistic or pessimistic?

3 Which things in the poem make *you* happy? Tell a partner, and add three more things that make you happy.

4 Cross out the word or phrase in each group which you cannot use with the verb.

Example: *You can listen to*   music
                    a dog
                    ~~a sauna~~
                    a story

4. You can tell   a speech
                 a story
                 the time
                 a joke

1. You can have   a party
                ten years old
                a baby
                a sauna

5. You can get   a phone call
                 a baby
                 a job
                 a cold

2. You can start   a car
                a job
                a lesson
                an illness

6. You can watch   a suspense film
                 a play
                 a football match
                 a photo

3. You can look at   old photographs
                 a car
                 a football match
                 a picture

7. You can make   a photo
                 friends
                 a mistake
                 a cake

5 Study the correct word partnerships in Exercise 4, then test your partner. (Your partner mustn't look at the book.)

Example: YOU: *Can you watch a play?*
      YOUR PARTNER: *Yes, you can.*
            YOU: *Can you make a photo?*
      YOUR PARTNER: *No, you can't.*

6 Write five sentences using the word partnerships to read to your partner. Your partner must ask you a question in response to each sentence. Answer it.

Example: YOU: *I had a sauna last night.*
      YOUR PARTNER: *Did you enjoy it?*
         YOU: *Yes, it was great.*

1 What makes you angry, or gets you annoyed? Write four sentences of your own, using these constructions:

It makes me angry when people are rude.
I get annoyed when I'm in a traffic jam and I'm late for a meeting.

Move around the room and compare your sentences. Which is the most common problem?

2 Some psychologists and scientists believe that these things can improve your mood in different ways:

exercise   colour   music   food and drink   positive thinking

In small groups, choose two and say if they help you beat a bad mood.

3 ▭▭ Listen to the recording and complete the table. Do you agree with any of the ideas?

	How they help
1. exercise	*Uses the oxygen you breathe in a good way and is better than drugs.*
2. colour	....
3. music	....
4. food and drink	....
5. positive thinking	....

4 Read the text and look at the pictures. What's the problem?

Dear Sir or Madam

I am enclosing some photos of my office where I employ a small workforce of ten people. They are a nice group of people, but at the end of the day everyone seems to go home in a bad mood. They get annoyed with each other and with me, and seem bored and depressed by the working environment.
I think it must be the environment, because the work itself is interesting and each person has their own area of responsibility.
    What can I do to improve the situation before my staff start leaving?
    I look forward to hearing from you.
        Yours faithfully
            Chris Young

5 Work in groups. Suggest how to improve the situation in this office. Here is a construction to help you:

Examples **They could** *have a meeting to talk about their feelings.*
           They could *get some nice pictures to put on the walls.*

When you have finished, report your ideas to the class.

PERSONAL STUDY WORKBOOK

In your Personal Study Workbook, you will find more exercises to help you with your learning. For Unit 10, these include:

- further practice with -*ing* forms and infinitives
- a vocabulary exercise on different uses of *get*
- quotations by famous people about happiness
- a pronunciation dictation exercise
- the next page of your visual dictionary – likes/dislikes, verb + noun collocations

---

REVIEW AND DEVELOPMENT

REVIEW OF UNIT 8

1 Words often confused   vocabulary

Underline the correct word or words in brackets in these sentences.

1. I'm going out this evening, so I need a babysitter to (look for/look after) the children.
2. This dress doesn't (fit/suit) me; I need a bigger size.
3. You could get your sister a nice present at the (library/bookshop).
4. Could you (lend/borrow) me some money?
5. If you're hot you can (put off/take off) your sweater.
6. Do you ever (use/wear) training shoes?
7. I went to the shop to (bring/take) my trousers back.
8. You must be careful what you say to him because he is very (sensible/sensitive).
9. The phone (fare/bill) is quite high.
10. We can go (on/by) foot.

Can you use the other words correctly?

2 Asking questions   social situations: shops

A Work in small groups. You have four minutes to do this exercise.
Make a list of ten questions you could ask in a clothes shop when you are buying something to wear, or taking it back.

Example: *Could I try this on, please?*

Now list five questions the assistant could ask you.

Example: *Could I see your receipt?*

B ▭ Listen to the recording. Write down any questions which are different from yours. Did you think of questions which aren't on the recording? Tell the group.

REVIEW OF UNIT 9

1 You should boil it | have to, don't have to; mustn't and should(n't) |

Work in small groups. Write five sentences about food, using the structures above. You can use the vocabulary below or make your own sentences.

Example: *You have to cook rice before you eat it.*
You shouldn't keep biscuits in a warm place.

boil
cook   eat
peel   reheat
wash
keep

Tell your ideas to the rest of the group.

2 I keep it in my wallet | vocabulary |

If you *keep* something somewhere, it means you put it somewhere so that you can look after it, and because you will need it sometimes.

Example: *You keep money in a bank account, to keep it safe, or because you can get interest from it.*

Look at the list of words. Where do you keep these things, and why? (If you like, you can say, 'It's a secret where I keep it!')

milk
your sunglasses/glasses
records/cassettes/CDs
your wallet/purse
photos
your passport/identity card
your cheque book/credit cards
your bicycle/car

3 Going to restaurants | speaking |

With a partner, think of at least ten reasons why people decide to eat in restaurants.

Examples: *The company is paying.*
You're going to the cinema and you haven't got time to go home to eat.

When you have finished, compare your list with another pair.

11

WEATHER

Language focus:	Vocabulary:
too and *very*;	weather
enough, *too much* and *too many*	jobs
quantifiers: *a lot*, *a bit*, etc.	consumer goods
verb patterns: *keep*, *stop*	
can to express known facts	

IT KEEPS YOU COOL
weather vocabulary; verb patterns: *can*

1 Some people have strong reactions to the weather. What about you? Find out how other members of the group often feel:

- on a cold winter's morning.
- on a warm summer's evening with a gentle sea breeze.
- on a hot summer's day.
- on a wet and windy day.
- towards the end of a long spell of very hot humid weather.
- just before a violent thunderstorm.

  Now listen to some people giving their opinions. What do they feel? Make notes.

2 Match the pictures with the words.

suntan lotion   winter boots   an umbrella
air conditioning   a fan   central heating

3 Look at these sentences: It *keeps you cool* in hot weather.
(to keep somebody/something + adjective)

They *stop your feet getting* cold.
(to stop something *–ing*)

It *can mark* your clothes.
They *can be* very noisy.
(can + verb)

Write the four sentences above in the correct spaces (positive or negative) in the following table.

	Positive (+)	Negative (-)
umbrellas	....	....
fans	....	....
central heating	....	....
suntan lotion	....	....
winter boots	....	....
air conditioning	It keeps you cool in hot weather.	....
....	....	....

4 Now work with a partner. Write more positive and negative sentences in the table, using the structures above.

Compare your answers in small groups. Add one more example to the list in the table, and ask a new partner about its positive and negative features.

5 Which are the two most important things from the table in your daily life? Discuss in groups and say why.

ARE YOU HAPPY WITH YOUR WEATHER? *too, very; enough, too much, too many*

1 Look at the picture. What is the difference between *too* and *very*?

Are these summer temperatures hot, very hot or too hot for you?
What about the winter temperatures?
Are they cold, very cold or too cold for you?

Summer temperatures (°C)	Winter temperatures (°C)
25° 35° 45°	10° 0° –10°

It's very hot, isn't it?

It's too hot for me!

2 Think about the weather in your country and put a tick (✓) beside the comments you agree with.

It's too cold in the winter.
The weather is very changeable.
There isn't enough variety.
It's too windy.
There are too many thunderstorms.
There's too much fog in the winter.
It's too hot in the summer.
It's very humid in the summer.
There isn't enough snow in the winter.
There's too much rain.
There isn't enough rain in the summer
    and everything gets very dry.
It isn't hot enough in the summer.

Compare your answers in groups.

3 Look at the use of *too*, *too much*, *too many* and *enough* in the exercise above, and then decide if the following sentences are right or wrong. If they are wrong, correct them. Compare your answers with a partner.

1. We couldn't see the church because it was too foggy.
2. I didn't go out because I was too much tired.
3. I don't like it when there is too much rain.
4. There were too much people on the bus, so we got off.
5. I didn't have enough money to go to the restaurant.
6. He said the soup wasn't enough hot, but mine was OK.
7. I didn't get the job because my English wasn't good enough.
8. There wasn't enough space on the bus and it was too slow.
9. Have you got enough eggs to make the cake?

4 Complete the sentences in the box, using *too*, *enough*, *too many* or *too much*. Then compare with a partner. If you prefer, look at the rules on page 164 and then do the exercise.

.... can go before adjectives like *hot* and *slow*.
.... can go after adjectives like *hot* and *slow*.
.... can go before nouns like *books* and *time*.
.... can go before uncountable nouns like *fog* and *rain*.
.... can go before countable nouns like *storms* and *days*.

5 In groups, write a description of your ideal climate in the table below. Consider the following: temperature   rainfall   humidity   seasonal differences.

Jan–Mar	Apr–Jun	Jul–Sep	Oct–Dec

Tell the rest of the class what your group thinks.

WEATHER AND THE ECONOMY

1 Look at the list of jobs in the table below. Does the weather affect these people:

– a lot?
– quite a lot?
– a bit?
– not at all?

Give your reasons. Compare your answers with a partner.

Job	How much?	How?
pilot	a lot	It affects the route and speed of the plane; a pilot cannot fly in bad weather.
photographer	a bit	A photographer may use different film, or take pictures of different things in different seasons.
supermarket manager		
fashion model		
firefighter		
author		
chemist/pharmacist		

What other jobs are affected by the weather, and how? Discuss in groups.

ARE YOU HAPPY WITH YOUR WEATHER?   73

2 📼 Listen to a journalist talking about the effect of the weather on supermarket sales. Complete the sentences and then compare them with a partner.

	Product		*When?*
Sales of	..coffee...........	go up / rise	.in wet weather.............. .
	....		....
	....		....
	....		....
	....		....
	....		....

Do any of them surprise you? Do you think it is the same in your country?

3 How do the different seasons affect the sales of the following goods? (a lot? quite a lot? not much? not at all?) Discuss in groups.

ice cream   perfume   towels   candles
socks   light bulbs   writing paper   batteries
lemons   T-shirts   washing powder
vinegar   video recorders   short-sleeved shirts
hats   antiseptic cream   blankets

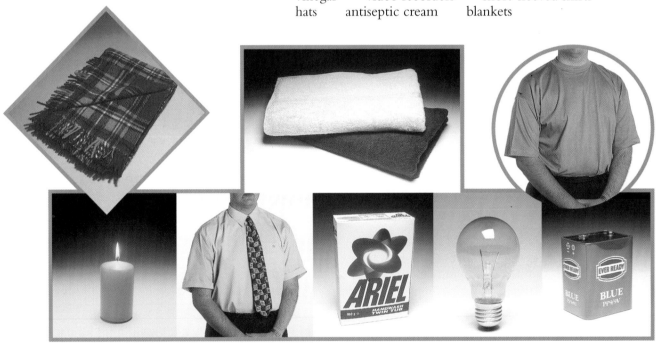

4 In your groups, write four more products like the ones in Exercise 3 and pass them to another group to discuss.

PERSONAL STUDY WORKBOOK

In your Personal Study Workbook, you will find more exercises to help you with your learning. For Unit 11, these include:

- exercises to practise *too, enough, too much, too many*
- vocabulary revision
- a listening passage about a strange illness related to the weather
- a reading text on folklore about the weather
- another page of your visual dictionary – weather

REVIEW OF UNIT 9

1 That sounds different [pronunciation]

⊂⊃ In the groups below, the underlined vowel sound in one word is pronounced differently from the others. Find the odd one out, then listen and check your answers.

Example: *drunk   mustard   full   duck*   *The answer is* full.

1. salad   bacon   cabbage   carrot
2. cook   food   spoon   room
3. peach   meal   beans   healthy
4. menu   lettuce   refuse   cucumber
5. diet   recipe   fried   pineapple
6. pork   cork   fork   work

2 Food [vocabulary]

Here are some 'general' words. How many examples can you think of for each one? Work with a partner.

1. Meat: ...*beef, lamb*...........................
2. Cutlery: ....
3. Dairy products: ....

This is one simple way of organising and revising vocabulary. Can you find three more 'general' words connected with food and drink? Work with a partner and write down as many examples as you can for each one.

REVIEW OF UNIT 10

1 Feelings [vocabulary]

Answer the questions using the words in the box.

happy	angry	depressed	optimistic	pessimistic	worried
annoyed	bored (with)	satisfied (with)	excited	frightened (of)	

How do you feel about:
– your personal future?   – public transport in your country?
– your progress in English?   – politics?
– your country's future?   – pollution?

Compare your answers in small groups. Say why you feel the way you do. Then add two more topics to the list and ask people in the group how they feel about them.

2 Classifications [verbs and verb patterns]

Work with a partner and classify the verbs in the box in five different ways.

promise	intend	offer	regret	enjoy	refuse	decide	give up
can't stand	don't mind	would like	love	avoid	want	imagine
finish	hope	hate				

1. a. verbs which take *-ing*. Example: *enjoy*
   b. verbs which take the infinitive. Example: *promise*
   c. verbs which take either *-ing* or the infinitive. Example: *love*
2. Verbs which mean something to do with liking and not liking. Example: *enjoy*
3. Verbs which have a negative *idea*. Example: *refuse*
4. Verbs which often have something to do with the future. Example: *promise*
5. Verbs which are pronounced /ɪd/ as the past tense ending. Example: *intended*

12

ROMANCE

Language focus:
past continuous and past simple
link words: *when* and *while*
verb + preposition
prepositional phrases

Vocabulary:
physical scenery
relationships and romance

1 Here are some things which people often think are romantic. Do you agree, and have any of them ever happened to you or people you know? Discuss in groups.

– Candlelit dinners at home with your partner.
– Receiving presents from your partner for no special reason.
– Your partner organises a surprise party for you.
– You and your partner decide to go away on holiday tomorrow.
– You fall in love at first sight.

Think of two more romantic actions or scenes like these to ask people in your group about.

2 Some countries celebrate Valentine's Day. Can you answer any of these questions about it? If not, try to find someone in the group who can.

1. When is it?
2. What do people do on Valentine's Day?
3. What is the origin of it?

CD Listen to the recording and find out the answers to the questions above. Then compare your answers.

3 Answer these questions in small groups.

1. Do you have something similar in your own country? If so, how is it different?
2. When do people give presents or send cards?
3. Do you have: Mother's Day?　　Father's Day?　　Children's Day?　　Teacher's Day?
   Pet's Day?　　Grandparents' Day?
4. What other days do you celebrate?

4 Here are some typical Valentine's Day messages. Complete each of the rhymes and then compare your answers with a partner. Use a dictionary if necessary.

Example:　Roses are red,
　　　　　Violets are blue,
　　　　　Sugar is sweet,
　　　　　And so *are you* .

Roses are red, violets are blue.
My love for you will always ....

Even when I'm old and grey
I'll love you as much
As I do ....

I love you East,
I love you West,
But right here's where
I love ....

I'm yours tonight,
Will you be mine?
I love you
....

You make me feel
dazed, crazed, ecstatic and more.
You make me feel love
Like never ....

Roses are red,
The sky is blue,
And all that I need
Is to share ....

5 With a partner, try to make up another Valentine's Day rhyme. Compare your rhymes with other pairs and choose the best one in the class.

A FIRST MEETING
past continuous

1 Which of these can you see within a two-minute walk of where you are now?

a narrow path　　a bridge　　a valley　　a steep hill　　a lake　　a forest　　a lane

2 Read the story and discuss these questions with a partner.

1. What is the relationship between Madeleine and Andy?
2. What do you think is going to happen this evening?

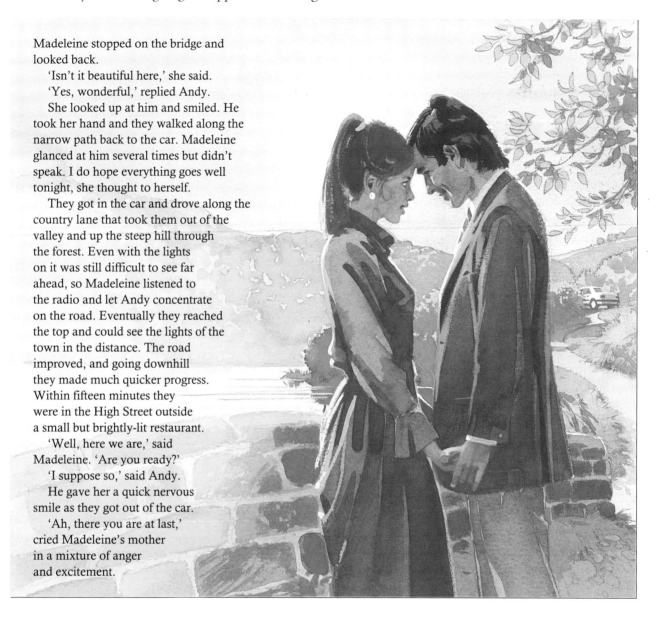

Madeleine stopped on the bridge and looked back.

'Isn't it beautiful here,' she said.

'Yes, wonderful,' replied Andy.

She looked up at him and smiled. He took her hand and they walked along the narrow path back to the car. Madeleine glanced at him several times but didn't speak. I do hope everything goes well tonight, she thought to herself.

They got in the car and drove along the country lane that took them out of the valley and up the steep hill through the forest. Even with the lights on it was still difficult to see far ahead, so Madeleine listened to the radio and let Andy concentrate on the road. Eventually they reached the top and could see the lights of the town in the distance. The road improved, and going downhill they made much quicker progress. Within fifteen minutes they were in the High Street outside a small but brightly-lit restaurant.

'Well, here we are,' said Madeleine. 'Are you ready?'

'I suppose so,' said Andy.

He gave her a quick nervous smile as they got out of the car.

'Ah, there you are at last,' cried Madeleine's mother in a mixture of anger and excitement.

3 The following five sentences have been removed from the story. Where should they go? Work with a partner.

1. Inside people *were talking* and laughing.
2. Across the road a middle-aged couple *were waving* frantically.
3. The sun *was setting* over the lake and trees were swaying gently in the warm air.
4. She could see he *was thinking* about the meeting later that evening.
5. It *was getting* quite dark now and the lane was very narrow.

4 Most of the story is in the past simple, but the sentences above all include verbs in the past continuous (*was/were* + *-ing*).

Look at these two sentences:

Madeleine *stopped* on the bridge and *looked* back.
The sun *was setting* over the lake.

Can you see a difference in meaning between the past simple and the past continuous? Discuss with a partner, then check in the Grammar Reference on page 165.

5 Test your understanding of the difference. Underline the correct word or words in brackets in these sentences.

1. The alarm went off and she (jumped/was jumping) out of bed. She (put on/was putting on) a pair of shorts ready to go to the beach, then she (looked/was looking) out of the window and saw that it (rained/was raining).

2. He (washed/was washing) his hair when suddenly he (heard/was hearing) a noise. He (ran/was running) downstairs and (opened/was opening) the back door. His niece (sat/was sitting) on the doorstep with a small kitten in her hand.

3. When she (went/was going) into the cinema it (poured/was pouring) with rain, but when she (came/was coming) out the sun (shone/was shining) so she (went/was going) for a walk in the park.

4. We (arrived/were arriving) fifteen minutes before the play was scheduled to start, but already the theatre (filled up/was filling up) and people in the audience (talked/were talking) noisily.

5. I (sat/was sitting) down and (ordered/was ordering) a drink. Three men (played/were playing) cards in one corner of the bar, but I was fairly certain that none of them (recognised/was recognising) me.

6 With your partner, construct the story about Madeleine and Andy again (including the five sentences from Exercise 3), but this time make some changes:

– Change the names of the people.　　– Change the season.
– Change the place.　　– Change the reason why the couple are nervous.
– Change the time of day.

Now tell your story to a different partner.

SHORT BUT SWEET　　link words; prepositions

1 Have you got a holiday romance story about yourself or a friend?
Tell your stories in groups.

2 ▭▭ Listen to this holiday romance and answer these questions.

1. Where does the story take place?
2. Why is the speaker attracted to the other person?
3. Does the story end happily? Why or why not?

Compare your answers with a partner.

3 Read this true story and finish the last line yourself.

An English friend of mine, Ian, was staying with friends in America. One night, while he was having a drink in a bar, he met an English woman called Jane. They spent a lot of time together during Ian's holiday and got on very well, but when he left he didn't write down Jane's address in England.

Two months later, in August, when Ian was relaxing on holiday in Corfu, he met an Irish woman called Elizabeth. They had a great time together and at the end of the holiday they exchanged addresses. By coincidence, Elizabeth lived very close to Ian's parents in Manchester, so when he went to visit them in October, he decided to call on Elizabeth at the same time. He rang the bell to her flat, but when the door opened …

Compare your answer with a partner. Your teacher will tell you how the story ended.

4 Look at these sentences from the first paragraph of the story:

1. While he was having a drink, he met an English woman …
2. When he left, he didn't write down Jane's address …

In the first example, you can use *when* or *while*, because they both mean *during the period of time*.

In the second example, you cannot use *while*, because we aren't talking about a period of time, but a single action.

Look at the second paragraph of the story. When can you use *while* in place of *when*?

5 Work with a partner. One of you is Ian, the other is Jane. Think about these questions and then act out the conversation that takes place when Jane opens the door.

Jane	*Ian*
What can you remember about Ian?	What can you remember about Jane?
What do you feel about him?	What do you feel about her?
Are you expecting to see him?	Are you expecting to see her?
Why do you think he has come?	Why do you think she is there?
What are your first words?	What are your first words?

6 There are many verbs in English that are followed by a preposition, and many phrases that include a preposition.

Examples: *It **depends on** the weather.*
*We got there **in time**.*

Complete the following sentences with the correct preposition.

1. I hardly ever *listen* ...... the radio.
2. When I was a teenager I *fell* ...... love every week.
3. What are you *thinking* ...... ?
4. They went away ...... *holiday* a couple of days ago.
5. When we turned the corner I could see the church ...... *the distance.*
6. ...... *coincidence* we both chose the same dress.
7. I *glanced* ...... my watch and realised it was time to go.
8. It was *pouring* ...... *rain* when we left.

All the answers are in the unit, so go back and check if you can't remember any of them.

PERSONAL STUDY WORKBOOK

In your Personal Study Workbook, you will find more exercises to help you with your learning. For Unit 12, these include:

- an exercise to test your understanding of the past simple and continuous
- a sentence building exercise using vocabulary and link words
- love letters to read
- an exercise on prepositions
- poems to read and write

REVIEW AND DEVELOPMENT

REVIEW OF UNIT 10

1 Listen and answer | vocabulary |

☐☐ Listen and write down your answers. Then look at Tapescript 9 on page 174.

Read the questions to a partner. Can they answer all of them?

2 Tell me the truth | verbs and verb patterns |

Write down four different things:

you can start   e.g. *a lesson, a car, a journey, a job*
you can make
you can tell

And three things: And two things: And something:

you can't avoid   you don't mind   that keeps you warm
you can't imagine   you don't regret   that keeps you dry
you can't stand   you don't enjoy   that keeps you healthy

Compare your answers in groups.

REVIEW OF UNIT 11

1 I love walking in the rain | -ing forms and weather vocabulary |

A Put these phrases in order:

> I like   I'm not very keen on   I don't mind
> I love   I quite like   I can't stand

B Complete the sentences using the phrases above. If you have no experience of these weather conditions, you can say so.

Examples: *I can't stand*   *travelling in bad weather.*
            I have no experience of *making snowmen.*

1. .... lying in the sun.
2. .... flying during a thunderstorm.
3. .... going out when it is windy.
4. .... walking in the rain.
5. .... driving on icy roads.
6. .... eating outside on warm summer evenings.
7. .... getting wet.
8. .... being outside during a snowstorm.

Compare your answers in groups.

2 Haiku | writing and pronunciation |

A *haiku* is a 3-line Japanese poem which consists of seventeen syllables: 5 in the first line, 7 in the second and 5 in the third. Here are two written by learners of English which won prizes in a haiku competition. Read them and count the syllables.

The wind comes slowly
And the leaves fall on the grass.
Autumn has arrived.

Cristina Molina Cedres, The Canary Islands

The engine was green
It was a hot summer day
We left the station.

Thomas Allinger, Australia

The judge in the competition was Wendy Cope, a British poet and critic, and she has written many haiku herself. Here are some of her comments:

> The essential idea of the haiku is to observe the world and express one moment in it. The writers of the best haiku understand that a good poem must 'please the ear'. The poem by Cristina Molina Cedres (above) is very attractive because it is so simple.
>
> The most common mistake in other haiku in the competition was that people forgot words, usually articles or pronouns, that would not be omitted in normal spoken English. The absence of little words like 'the' and 'my' and 'and' can be terrible for the music of the poem.

Here are some more examples of haiku about the weather. Complete them in a suitable way. Compare your version with a partner.

The morning .... lifts
And so once more I can see
the .... in the ....

A flash of ....
is soon followed by thunder:
the ....

Now write a haiku about the weather. Remember to count the syllables.

13

IT'S BETTER TO TRAVEL THAN TO ARRIVE

Language focus:	Vocabulary:
plural nouns	airports and flying
countable and uncountable nouns	travel: verb + noun collocations
requests and enquiries	

LET'S GET ORGANISED!

1 Do you organise everything in advance? Do you leave everything till the last minute? Are you in between? Put a cross on the line.

'last-minute' _____ long-term
    traveller   planner

Compare your answers in small groups.

2 Use the pictures and a dictionary to check that you understand the vocabulary in the table.

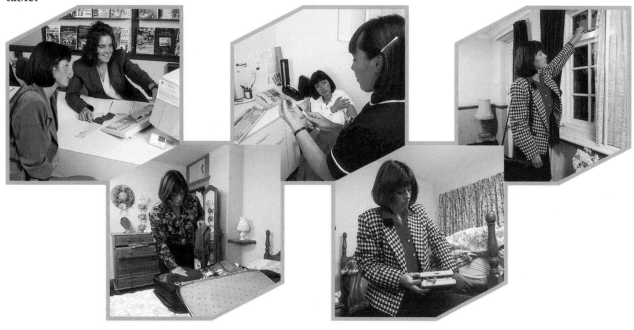

A few weeks before	The day before	One hour before leaving home
do your packing	have injections	check your passport is in order
book the flight	take out travel insurance	turn off the gas and electricity
buy a suitcase	arrange accommodation	check the doors and windows
make a list of things to do	get a visa	call for a taxi
	arrange for someone	hide any valuables
	to look after your pet	get a guidebook
		get foreign currency

Work with a partner. Are the events in the table logical at these times?

Example: *You normally have injections weeks before, not the day before you travel.*

3 ⬚⬚ ⬚⬚ Listen to a woman describing some of the preparations she made for a journey. Tick (✓) the things in the table she talks about.

Now listen again. When did she do each of these things?

4 Work in small groups. Tell each other about the preparations you made for your last big journey.

5 Look at the following sentence:

When you do your packing, do you take *trousers* and/or *jeans*?

The nouns *trousers* and *jeans* only have a plural form and you must use the plural form of a verb with them:

Examples: *My trousers **are** dirty.* (not 'my trouser is')
*I need **some** jeans.* (not 'a jeans')
*Her clothes **look** beautiful on her.* (not 'looks')

Often with items of clothing, you want to refer to a specific number. Use *some, a pair of,* or a number:

Examples: *I bought some trousers / a pair of trousers.*
I bought seven pairs of trousers.

The words in this list all end in 's', but which ones *always* end in 's'?

jeans	glasses	pyjamas
shoes	shorts	underpants
pants	socks	scissors
sunglasses	gloves	swimming trunks
bikinis	binoculars	tights

6 Imagine you are going on your favourite type of holiday. How many things from the above list would be in your suitcase? If you like, compare your answers with someone of the opposite sex.

AIRPORTS
uncountable nouns; airport vocabulary

1 Discuss in small groups.

– When did you last go to an airport?
– Why did you go there?
– Which airport was it, and what was it like?
– Have you been to any other airports? If so, what were they like?

2 Do this quiz in the same groups. Use a dictionary if necessary.

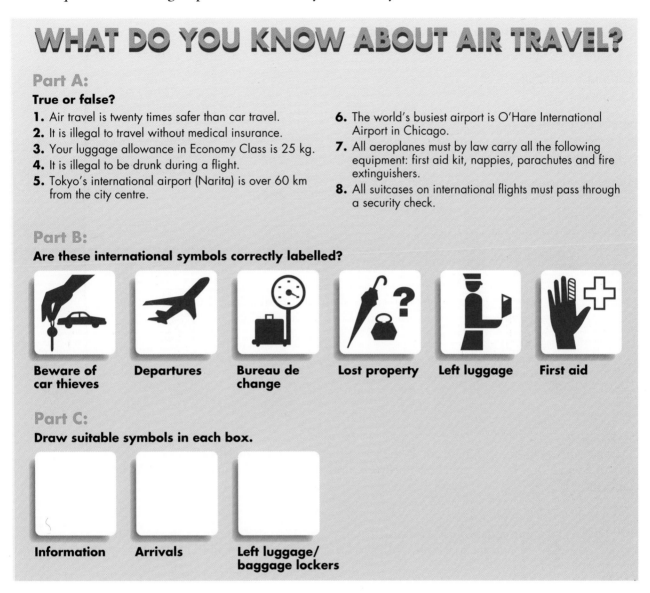

WHAT DO YOU KNOW ABOUT AIR TRAVEL?

Part A:
True or false?

1. Air travel is twenty times safer than car travel.
2. It is illegal to travel without medical insurance.
3. Your luggage allowance in Economy Class is 25 kg.
4. It is illegal to be drunk during a flight.
5. Tokyo's international airport (Narita) is over 60 km from the city centre.
6. The world's busiest airport is O'Hare International Airport in Chicago.
7. All aeroplanes must by law carry all the following equipment: first aid kit, nappies, parachutes and fire extinguishers.
8. All suitcases on international flights must pass through a security check.

Part B:
Are these international symbols correctly labelled?

Beware of car thieves | Departures | Bureau de change | Lost property | Left luggage | First aid

Part C:
Draw suitable symbols in each box.

Information | Arrivals | Left luggage/ baggage lockers

Check your answers with the teacher. Did any answers surprise you?

3 Look at these sentences.

We had wonderful <u>weather</u> on our holiday.

She gave us some good <u>advice</u> about places to visit.

The nouns underlined are *uncountable*: you cannot make them plural (by adding 's') and they are not used with the indefinite article (*a* or *an*).

Which nouns in the box below are countable, and which are uncountable? A dictionary will tell you if you are not sure.

weath·er¹ /'weðəʳ/ *n* [U] **1** the condition of wind, rain, sunshine, snow, etc., at a certain time or over a period of time: *good weather|What will the weather be like tomorrow?*
(from *Longman Active Study Dictionary of English*)

advice /ɔ³dvaɪs/. **1** If you give someone **advice**, you tell them what you think they should do in a particular situation. EG *She promised to follow his advice... They want advice on how to do it... One woman went to a psychiatrist for advice.*   N UNCOUNT : USU +SUPP / ↑ help / = counsel
(from *Collins COBUILD English Language Dictionary*)

travel   journey   suitcase   insurance   information   trip
equipment   luggage   first aid   baggage   flight   air

Do you have countable or uncountable words in your own language? If so, are the words in the box countable or not?

4 Work with a partner. Complete each sentence to give a total of 10 words (not 9 or 11!) and use an uncountable noun in each one. Contractions count as one word.

Example: *I need to* .get more information from the travel agency....

1. I went to ....
2. I must remember ....
3. I'm looking for ....
4. Have you got ....?
5. I couldn't ....
6. I asked her ....

Compare your examples with another pair.

1 Problems often start when passengers arrive at their destination in a foreign country. Can you add two more examples to this list? Work with a partner.

1. Your luggage is missing.
2. A customs officer stops you as you are walking through the 'Nothing to Declare' door.
3. You don't know how to get to the centre of the city.
4. You have to hire a car at the airport for a few days.
5. ....
6. ....

Imagine you are in these situations. Which is the easiest and which is the most difficult, when you have to speak *in English*? Compare in small groups and say *why* you think so.

2 In which of the four situations in Exercise 1 could you hear the questions in the table below? And who would be speaking? (More than one answer is possible.)

– passenger
– customs officer
– airline representative
– car hire representative
– someone who works at the airport information desk

	Number of situation	Speaker
1. Does this belong to you?	1, 2	airline representative, customs officer
2. Could you describe it for me?		
3. Could I see your licence?		
4. Sorry to bother you, but could you tell me ...?		
5. How long will it take?		
6. Could you fill in this form, please?		
7. Excuse me, could you open your suitcase?		
8. Can you deliver it when it arrives?		
9. Can I have one straightaway?		
10. How often do they run?		

Compare with a partner.

3 With your partner, choose one of the situations in Exercise 1 (or one of your own, if you prefer) and write a conversation (6–8 lines). Include any useful questions from the list in Exercise 2.

Practise your conversation together and learn it by heart. Then act your sketch for the others in the class.

PERSONAL STUDY WORKBOOK

In your Personal Study Workbook, you will find more exercises to help you with your learning. For Unit 13, these include:

- exercises to revise travel vocabulary and phrasal verbs
- a correction activity for uncountable nouns
- reading travel advice from Queen Elizabeth II
- writing postcards
- the next page of your visual dictionary – at an airport

REVIEW AND DEVELOPMENT

REVIEW OF UNIT 11

1 It's too heavy and I'm not strong enough

> *too* and *enough*; vocabulary

Complete the sentences using *too* or *enough* plus a suitable adjective from this list.

strong	loud	deep	shallow	hard	easy	difficult	light
dark	heavy	soft	icy	young	old	ill	weak

Example: *I couldn't carry the suitcase because* **it was too heavy**.
or   *I couldn't carry the suitcase because* **I wasn't strong enough**.

1. We couldn't talk in the disco because the music ....
2. I couldn't drink the coffee because it ....
3. She couldn't get out of bed because she ....
4. They all failed because the exam ....
5. We couldn't swim because the water ....
6. He couldn't join the club because he ....
7. I couldn't drive because the roads ....
8. We couldn't play because the ground ....

2 Sounds similar | pronunciation |

▭ Read the sentences and then listen to the recording. Are the sentences you hear the same or different? Underline any differences and change them.

1. It's often foggy in the winter.
2. We don't have ice on the roads in winter.
3. Do you get a lot of sun in spring?
4. We had a showery March.
5. I love the misty mornings in spring.
6. We get a lot of winds in the autumn.
7. Did you say it was cloudy outside?
8. We had a horrible thundery night in the mountains.

Now test your partner. Read the sentences above but do what the person did in the recording – change two of them. Can your partner hear which ones?

REVIEW OF UNIT 12

1 What was going on? | past continuous |

Complete the situations using the past continuous.

Example: *I looked out of the window.* **The sun was shining**, *so I decided to get dressed and go for a walk.*

1. I looked out of the window. ...., so I went back to bed.
2. I looked out of the window. ...., so I rang the police immediately.
3. I looked out of the window. ...., so I shouted 'Good morning', and waved.
4. I looked out of the window. ...., so I told her to pick them up and put them in a litter bin.
5. I looked out of the window. ...., so I asked him if he wanted any help.
6. I looked out of the window. ...., so I told him to get off and leave it alone.
7. I looked out of the window. ...., so I put on some clothes and went downstairs to let her in.
8. I looked out of the window. ...., so I moved back and put a shirt on immediately.

2 Get dressed and put on your jacket | vocabulary |

Do Exercise A while a partner does Exercise B on page 171. Then compare your answers.

A Complete the following sentences with a suitable verb, phrase or adjective.

1. It was getting cold so I .... my jacket.
2. He's getting very .... because he's taking his driving test next week.
3. It was getting dark so I .... the light.
4. It was getting quite warm so I .... my jacket.
5. He doesn't celebrate birthdays so much now that he's getting ....
6. He was getting fat so I told him to .... a diet.
7. He takes a lot of exercise so he's getting quite ....
8. It was getting late and I'm afraid I .... asleep.

14

POSSESSIONS

| Language focus: present perfect vs. simple past (3) *for* and *since* *how long?* | Vocabulary: possessions class words, e.g. jewellery, pets household objects and appliances |

MY FAVOURITE THINGS   present perfect; superordinates

1 📼 Listen to these two people talking about important possessions and correct the texts while you listen.

guess the thing which is most important to me is my grandfather's watch. My mother gave it to me on my eighteenth birthday, so I've had it now for thirty years. What's more, I think I've worn it every day. It has great sentimental value and would be difficult to replace because it has been in the family since before the First World War.

ell, I'm a great jazz fan, and I have a really large collection of records – well over four thousand – which is very important to me. I started buying records when I was at school, but I've only been a serious collector since 1980 – that's when I left university and started earning money. And I guess that most of the records I've had for fifteen years are impossible to replace, so I'd hate to lose any.

Read your corrected texts to a partner and make sure you agree.

2 Underline the examples of the present perfect in the two texts. Which diagram below best describes the meaning? Can you also see the difference between *for* and *since* in the examples?

A   NOW   B   NOW   C   NOW
PAST   PAST   PAST

---

3 Write down one of your most important possessions and think about the following questions:

- Where did you get it?
- How long have you had it?
- Why is it important?
- Could you replace it easily?

Tell at least six people about your important possession, and make a list of their possessions.

4 Work with a partner. How many of the possessions in your lists can be classified under the following headings? Use a dictionary to help you.

jewellery
pets
toys
musical instruments
articles of clothing
electrical appliances
forms of transport
sports equipment

Now look at the possessions you cannot classify under these headings. Can you classify them under other headings?

WE HAVEN'T SEEN EACH OTHER FOR YEARS present perfect

1 Look at the headline, the photos and the first paragraph from a newspaper article. What is a possible explanation for this story?

They haven't seen each other for 67 years

– but now reunited by their big bushy eyebrows!

Long lost brothers Bill and Buddy Robinson haven't seen each other for 67 years, but they are about to meet up – thanks to their distinctive bushy eyebrows!

2 Put the rest of the paragraphs in the correct order. Was your explanation correct?

a Since then, the two men have had long telephone conversations with each other but they will have to wait until next week when they can actually meet up.

b Then recently a miracle happened. Bill and his wife went to Canada, and needing cash, they stopped in a town and went into a bank. The bank cashier was Buddy's daughter, Gail!

c 'I saw that the man standing in front of me had the same bushy white eyebrows as my dad,' said Gail. Then she noticed that Bill's name was Robinson, the same as her dad, and they quickly realised he was her uncle.

d The incredible story began when the boys' mother ran away from home in Canada with her younger son, Buddy, leaving behind Bill, who was five at the time. She never contacted the family again, and never told Buddy he had a brother.

e However, Bill still remembered, and when he grew up and moved to America, he spent many years trying to find his brother and mother, but without success.

3 Now answer these questions. Tell a partner.

1. Why haven't Bill and Buddy seen each other for 67 years?
2. How did Bill find Buddy in the end?

4 Here are some more unusual situations. How many explanations can you think of for each one? Work with a partner.

Example: *He hasn't had a bath for ten years.*
Possible explanations: 1. *He always has a shower.*
                       2. *He has been a tramp for ten years.*

1. He hasn't driven his car for three years.
2. She hasn't worn her fur coat since 1993.
3. He hasn't used his electric shaver since 1990.
4. She hasn't bought any clothes since 1992.
5. He hasn't used a pen since he left school.
6. She hasn't been out of her house for twenty years.
7. He hasn't fed his pet rabbit for a month.
8. She hasn't played the flute for a week.

Explain your reasons to a different partner.

5 Now complete the following sentences about yourself. If necessary use the list of irregular verbs on page 175.

I haven't .... since the beginning of the lesson.
I haven't .... for two or three hours.
I haven't .... for three or four days.
I haven't .... since last year.
I haven't .... for a couple of years.
I haven't .... since I left school.

Say the first part of each of your sentences in a different order, and see if a partner can finish it with the correct time expression from the list.

Example: A: *I haven't washed my hair …*
         B: *Since last year?*
         A: *No, for three or four days.*

1 Read this description of a house. Choose the owner from the five pictures and complete the sentence below. Compare your answer with a partner.

FROM the lounge I get the

impression that this person is a bit of an intellectual. There is a large oak desk against one wall of the room, and a huge bookcase against the opposite wall. The desk is very untidy, and so is the rest of the room – empty cups on the coffee table and newspapers and magazines all over the floor. There's a very nice fireplace and in front of it, a very expensive-looking Persian rug with an armchair on one side and an old pair of slippers underneath.

The walls are covered in pictures that look very oriental – perhaps Chinese or Japanese, but the most surprising thing about the room is that there is a mobile phone, a calculator and an expensive computer, but no television in sight. And from my investigations, it appears that there isn't a TV anywhere in the house. What does that tell us?

I think this house belongs to ...... because ....
....
....

2 🔲 Now listen to the description of two more houses and choose the owners from the remaining four pictures. Write your answers here:

I think the first house belongs to ...... because ....
....

I think the second house belongs to ...... because ....
....

3 Work with a partner. Put the words in the box into the correct circles.

fur coat   hall   bedside table   lounge   drive   wardrobe   computer
calculator   oak desk   mobile phone   high-heeled shoes   fireplace
armchair   slippers   tracksuit   hi-fi   french windows   balcony
word processor   bookcase

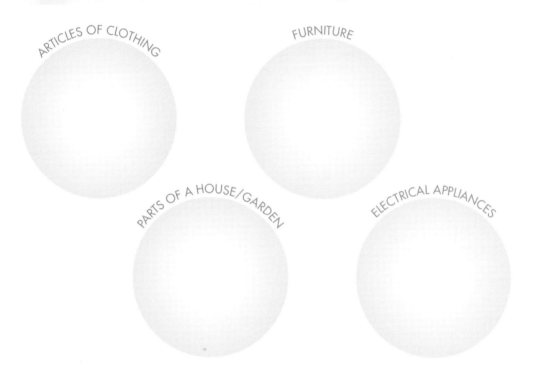

Which of these things do you have? If possible say where they are in your home.

Example: *I've got a pair of slippers which are normally in the bedroom.*
          I haven't got a fur coat.

4 Now write your own description of the house that belongs to one of the other two people in the pictures above.

Compare your description with someone who has written about the same person.

PERSONAL STUDY WORKBOOK

In your Personal Study Workbook, you will find more exercises to help you with your learning. For Unit 14, these include:

- an exercise to practise *for* and *since*
- a pronunciation activity on past participles
- vocabulary: an exercise on compound nouns, and another on electrical appliances
- reading and listening activities on problems with electrical goods
- another page of your visual dictionary – rooms and furniture

REVIEW OF UNIT 12

1 A story from the Middle East   reading and grammar

Before you begin this exercise, check that you understand these words:

liver (*noun*)   a hawk (*noun*)

Now read this story. There are seven mistakes in it. Correct the mistakes with a partner.

One day, a Khoja* buy some liver, and as he was carrying it away, he met a friend who asked how he were going to cook it.

'Oh, as usual,' he answered.

'No,' said his friend, 'there is a very nice way of do it. Let me describe it to you.'

He did so, but the Khoja said, 'I cannot remember all these details. Write down the recipe on a paper and I will cook the liver.'

His friend wrote it down and handed it to him.

He was going home, deep in thought, while a hawk flew down, took a liver out of his hand and flew off with it.

The Khoja, however, did not seem to be angry, for he held out the recipe and called to the hawk, 'What is the use of your doing that? You can't enjoy it, because I got the recipe here.'

* Khoja = a religious teacher in the Moslem faith

REVIEW OF UNIT 13

1 Air travel   vocabulary; requests and enquiries

Write down the following:

1. Three things in your house that you check just before you leave to go on holiday.
2. Three things you own that are checked by other people at the airport.
3. Three things that you might buy in the duty-free shop.
4. Three questions you might ask the flight attendant on the plane.
5. Three things that you do after the plane lands but before you get off the plane.
6. Three questions you might ask in the airport when you arrive.

Compare your answers in small groups.

2 Flight departures   listening

    Study the departures board for two minutes, then listen and answer the questions. There are some questions you cannot answer, so just write *I don't know*.

Remember, it's 3.00 pm (15.00 hrs) now.

15.00

FLIGHT NO	DEPARTURE TIME	DESTINATION	INFORMATION	GATE
MS 778	15.05	CAIRO	BOARDING FINAL CALL	21
UA 901	15.15	NEW YORK	BOARDING	13
BA 242	15.20	MEXICO CITY	DELAYED	
JL 402	15.25	TOKYO	BOARDING	22
TG 915	15.30	BANGKOK	DELAYED	
AA 87	15.35	CHICAGO		
VS 007	15.40	LOS ANGELES	BOARDING	14

RULES

Language focus:	Vocabulary:
if sentences with present tenses	verb + noun collocations
use of articles	social behaviour
past obligation/permission	geographical features

RULES OF BEHAVIOUR *if* sentences with present tenses; verb + noun collocations

The girl who ordered a glass of milk at the Café Royal

1 Look at the cartoon. Why are people shocked?

Can you think of a social rule in your country?
What do you think of it? Discuss in groups.

2 Demonstrate or mime these words and expressions with a partner.

to shake hands	to sneeze	to bow
to tap someone on the shoulder	to blow your nose	

Now match these verbs and
nouns to make expressions.

to wear	your turn
to make	someone 'sir' or 'madam'
to give	evening dress
to wait	someone a tip
to call	a phone call

Which of these actions do you do more than once a week? Tell your partner.

Example: *I probably shake hands with someone every day.*

3 Here are some social 'rules'. Imagine you are talking about Britain and choose the best sentence ending for each one. If you don't know an answer, have a guess.

If...

4 If someone next to you sneezes,
  a. it is the custom to say 'Jesus'.
  b. you can say 'Bless you'.

5 If you need to blow your nose,
  a. leave the room – never blow your nose in public.
  b. go ahead and do it.

6 If you are talking to a stranger who is older than you,
  a. call them 'sir' or 'madam'.
  b. don't call them anything.

7 If you go in a taxi,
  a. you normally give the driver a tip.
  b. you don't give the driver a tip.

8 If you are meeting someone for a drink,
  a. it is quite normal to arrive ten minutes late.
  b. it is very rude to arrive ten minutes late.

9 If you go into a bar for a drink,
  a. you can sit at a table and wait to be served.
  b. you have to go to the bar and pay for your drinks.

10 If you meet someone for the first time in a formal situation,
  a. it is normal to shake hands with them.
  b. you bow.

1 If you go to the theatre,
  a. you can wear what you like.
  b. you have to wear evening dress.

2 If someone is using a public phone box,
  a. it is OK to tap them on the shoulder and tell them you are waiting to make a call.
  b. you have to wait your turn.

3 If a person is sitting at a table in a coffee bar,
  a. it is OK for you to sit down at the same table if you ask permission.
  b. you should never sit down at the same table.

Compare your answers in small groups.

4 ▢▢ ▢▢ Listen to the recording. The two speakers are talking about Britain and Japan. Choose one of the speakers, and note down their answers to the questions above.

Find someone who chose the other speaker, and tell each other your answers.

5 Work in groups. If you are from the same country, make a list of useful rules of behaviour, using these structures:

If ...,   you can
          you should   } do this.
          you have to

If ...,   do this.
          don't do this.

Examples: *If you see an old person standing on a bus, you should give them your seat.*
           If you meet someone for the first time, don't kiss him or her.

If you are from different countries, go through the questions in Exercise 3 again, telling your group the customs of your country.

Do you know when we use *a, the* and no article in English? When do we say *a boy* and when *the boy*? There are quite a lot of rules, but you don't need to learn them all at once.

1 As you read the text, decide if the use of articles in English is the same as your mother tongue or different. (You could translate the examples to check this.) Compare your answers in small groups.

One of the most useful general rules about articles is this: we use *the* before a noun when the listener and speaker *know which thing or person they are talking about*. And we use *a* when we *don't know* which one, or when *it isn't important to know* which one.

Example:

I saw *a woman* in *the garden* this morning.
(We don't know which woman, but we know which garden.)

She started hitting *the tree* near *the front door*.
(We know which tree, because it refers to a specific one, and we know which door.)

I went and asked *the woman* what she was doing.
(We know *now* which woman, because the speaker talked about her before.)

Another important rule in English which is often different from other languages is about *things in general*. We don't use an article with plural nouns and uncountable nouns when we are talking about general categories: *all* fish or *all* dogs.

Compare: *Fish* is good for you. (all fish)
           I didn't like *the fish we had last night* very much.

           I couldn't sleep because of *the dogs next door*.
           Do you like *dogs*? (in general)

2 Now test your understanding of these rules. Complete the following short story with *a*, *the*, or no article.

When I got back to .... house, there was .... letter on .... doorstep addressed to my wife. Normally I don't open .... letters addressed to her, but I recognised .... handwriting so I decided to read it. Inside there was .... photograph and .... cheque for $1,000. I recognised .... photograph immediately but I was very surprised about .... money; it's not every day that .... cheques as big as that come through your letterbox.

Compare your answers with a partner.

Can you explain the story? Who is the photograph of? Why is there a cheque?

3 Work with a partner. One of you reads text A below, the other text B on page 171. Only read your own text. Add one more example to each category and then learn the information in your text. Shut your book and teach it to your partner.

Text A

We usually use *the* before:

rivers, oceans, seas
and mountain ranges

the Ganges,
the Pacific Ocean,
the Black Sea, the Andes,

....

groups of states or
groups of islands

the United States
*   of America,*
the Bahamas,

....

We *don't* usually use any article before:

lakes and mountains

Lake Como,
Mount Everest,

....

people's names

John Carter,
Mrs Barrett,

....

4 ⊡ Form small teams of 3–4. Listen to the quiz on the recording and decide on the answers together.

Your teacher will give you the answers. You score one point for each correct answer, and an extra point for each correct use of the article. The maximum is 20 points.

5 Discuss in groups.

- Is it useful to learn grammar rules?
- Do you enjoy it? Why? Why not?
- Do you know any grammar rules for your own language? Did you learn them at school? If so, was it useful?
- Do you think children should learn about the grammar of their own language?

1 Here are six rules. Correct them if they were not true of your secondary school.

Example: *We had to do homework every day.*

            didn't have to
    We ~~had to~~ do homework every day.

                           three times a week
    We had to do homework ~~every day~~.

1. We had to stand up when the teacher came into the room.

2. We didn't have to ask permission to leave the room.

3. We had to have lunch at school.

4. We didn't have to go to school on Saturdays.

5. We could call the teachers by their first names.

6. We couldn't talk to the person next to us.

Compare your answers in groups.

2 Using the pictures, and the structures in Exercise 1, write five more rules about your schooldays. Then tell a partner.

Example: *In my school we didn't have to sit in rows.*

3 📼 Listen to three people talking about the rules they had at school. Write down anything the speakers *had to do, didn't have to do,* or *couldn't do.*

4 Work in groups. Think about your childhood, and then tell others about some of the rules you had in your family.

Example: *We had to clean our room once a week.*

In the same groups, decide which of the rules you would like to continue with your own children, and which you wouldn't.

PERSONAL STUDY WORKBOOK

In your Personal Study Workbook, you will find more exercises to help you with your learning. For Unit 15, these include:

- exercises to revise articles and *had to* and *couldn't*
- activities to revise vocabulary collocations
- a quiz about language rules and a listening activity which gives you the answers
- a text from a book written in 1911 about social rules
- things to do with your speaking partner

REVIEW AND DEVELOPMENT

REVIEW OF UNIT 13

1 Silent letters   pronunciation

A Some letters in English words are not pronounced.

Examples: **k**nife, **w**rite

Underline the silent letters in these words.
(Do not include 'e' at the end of words.)

listen	know	thumb
knee	lamb	wrist
bomb	foreign	wrong
castle	island	whistle
fasten	sign	aisle

📼 Listen to the recording to check your answers, and repeat the words.

B Write at least five rules for yourself about silent letters in English, including this one:

The letter 'k' is silent in words beginning 'kn'.

2 International English   vocabulary

How many of the following English words and expressions are common in airports and planes in your own country?

tax-free	passport control	window seat	occupied	arrivals
out of order	boarding	baggage claim	aisle seat	self-service
gate	boarding card	emergency exit	fasten your seat belt	
check-in	departure lounge	nothing to declare		

Compare your answers with a partner and help each other with any words or expressions you don't know or can't remember.

3 Take off | vocabulary |

Complete the text with verbs from the box.

take off	get on	take out	stand up
look after	set off	check in	sit down
pick up	get off	turn off	fill in

First of all, when you are organising your trip you normally .... travel insurance and you may need to get someone to .... your house and/or pets while you are away. Then just before you leave your house and .... for the airport, you check that you have .... any dangerous electrical appliances. When you arrive you ...., and then you go through passport control and .... in the departure lounge. When your flight is called you .... the plane. If there are no delays, it normally .... about half an hour later. When you are in the air, you often have to .... an immigration form. After the plane lands and comes to a stop, you .... and .... the plane. Then you just have to go to the baggage claim where you .... your luggage.

REVIEW OF UNIT 14

1 Since last Tuesday | for or since? |

Do you use *for* or *since* with these time expressions?

a week	last Tuesday	three days
yesterday	ages	last night
two years	August	I was at school

Now complete these sentences about yourself, using *for* or *since* + a time expression.

1. Outside class, I haven't read anything in English ....
2. Outside class, I haven't listened to anything in English ....
3. Outside class, I haven't spoken in English ....
4. Outside class, I haven't written anything in English ....
5. Outside class, I haven't learnt any new vocabulary ....
6. Outside class, I haven't used a dictionary ....

Move round the class and compare your answers.

2 Lexical sets | vocabulary |

Read these sentences, complete them in a logical way, and then compare with a partner.

1. Jewellers sell necklaces, rings and ....
2. The place was full of musical instruments. He's got a guitar, a violin and ....
3. In my wardrobe, I've got a raincoat, two suits and ....
4. They love animals; they've got a dog, two cats and ....
5. I've owned a couple of cars, a racing bike and ....
6. In the bedroom there was just a bed, a wardrobe and ....
7. The kitchen appliances included a washing machine, a microwave and ....
8. The cupboard contained tennis rackets, football kit and ....

16

KEEPING THE CUSTOMER SATISFIED

Language focus:	Vocabulary:
will and *may/might* for predictions	adjectives describing character
if sentences (first conditional)	prefixes and word building
	money and business

CUSTOMER SERVICE

1 In places where people provide a service there is a common saying that 'the customer is always right'. Do you agree? Can you think of examples from your own experience? Discuss with a partner.

2 Divide these adjectives into words with a positive and negative meaning.

helpful   cold   impolite   knowledgeable   ignorant
efficient   smart   businesslike   badly dressed   rude

Positive	*Negative*
....	....
....	....
....	....
....	....
....	....

Discuss your answers with your teacher.

3 Work with a partner. Choose a specific example of one of these places that you both know well.

- a bank
- a post office
- a supermarket
- a clothes boutique
- a fast food restaurant
- the coffee bar/restaurant in your school

Now answer the questionnaire on your own. Don't consult your partner at this stage.

CUSTOMER SERVICE QUESTIONNAIRE

1. Speed of service
- ☐ a. Staff are usually slow and inefficient.
- ☐ b. Staff are reasonably efficient.
- ☐ c. Staff are very fast and efficient.
- ☐ d. Don't know / No experience.

2. Staff politeness
- ☐ a. Staff are sometimes rude.
- ☐ b. Staff can sometimes seem a bit impolite.
- ☐ c. Staff are very polite.
- ☐ d. Don't know / No experience.

3. Friendliness of staff
- ☐ a. Staff are sometimes cold and unfriendly.
- ☐ b. Staff are efficient and businesslike, but not very friendly.
- ☐ c. Staff are genuinely warm and friendly.
- ☐ d. Don't know / No experience.

4. Staff appearance
- ☐ a. Staff are badly dressed and don't seem to care about appearance.
- ☐ b. Staff look presentable, but could be smarter.
- ☐ c. Staff are very smart and well dressed.
- ☐ d. Don't know / No experience.

5. Helpfulness of staff
- ☐ a. Staff sometimes ignore you and keep you waiting.
- ☐ b. Staff serve you but are not very interested in you.
- ☐ c. Staff are genuinely helpful.
- ☐ d. Don't know / No experience.

6. Knowledge of products and services
- ☐ a. Staff seem fairly ignorant.
- ☐ b. Staff have a basic knowledge but no more.
- ☐ c. Staff are very knowledgeable.
- ☐ d. Don't know / No experience.

This questionnaire is based on a Customer Service Questionnaire issued to personal customers of Barclays Bank plc September 1992

Compare your answers with your partner. Do you have the same opinions?

4 Cover the questionnaire and then see if you can write down the opposites of these words. (Sometimes you need a prefix, e.g. 'un', 'in' or 'im', and sometimes you need a different word.)

polite   knowledgeable   efficient   warm   badly dressed   friendly

5 ▢▢ ▢▢ Listen to these people talking about good and bad service. Complete the table as you listen.

	Where?	Good or bad?	In what way?
Speaker 1			
Speaker 2			
Speaker 3			

6 Do staff need different qualities in different places? What are the most important qualities for staff in banks, clothes shops and fast food restaurants? Discuss in groups and then tell your answers to a different group.

1 Discuss these questions in groups.

1. Have you got a bank account? If so, what type is it?
2. Do you usually go to a bank for money or do you use cash machines?
3. How often do you take out money?

2 The man in the picture is a bank manager. He works in a very traditional bank in Scotland, but he has decided to change his image and wear casual clothes to work. Look at the possible consequences of his decision, and make sentences using *will*, *might* or *won't*.

Examples: *I think the bank will lose business.*
or *I think the bank may/might lose business.*
or *I don't think the bank will lose business.*
or *The bank won't (will not) lose business.*

CONSEQUENCES

Bank	*Employees*	*Customers*	*Bank manager*
lose business	start wearing casual clothes	be upset	get into trouble
get more young customers	think it's funny	complain	lose his job
....	....	....	....

Discuss your answers with a partner.

3 Can you add one more possible consequence to each category? Compare your answers in groups.

4 In your groups, choose one or two of the following situations and make a list of the possible consequences.

1. The Johnsons are a family of mother, father, sixteen-year-old son and two daughters, aged thirteen and eleven. One day the two daughters decide to become vegetarian. How will this affect the family?

2. The owner of a bar has decided not to permit smoking on Mondays, Wednesdays, Fridays and Sundays. How will this affect the bar?

3. A company which makes hearing aids has decided to stop the system of individual job responsibilities. When they arrive at work, staff decide what job they want to do. Of course, people cannot do certain jobs if they do not have the technical qualifications – but an engineer will be able to do marketing, and an economist will be able to show people how to use a new hearing aid. How will this affect the company and the relationships within it?

Compare your answers with other groups. Which consequences are the most common, and which consequence is the most interesting from the different groups?

5 ▭ Listen to some people talking about situations two and three. Do they have the same ideas as you did? If not, write them down.

A NEW APPROACH
if sentences with *will, may, might*

1 Work with a partner. Look at the example and then change the other sentences to make them logical.

Example: *If we take a taxi to the station, it'll be cheaper.*
If we take a <u>bus</u> to the station, it'll be cheaper.
If we <u>don't</u> take a taxi to the station, it'll be cheaper.

1. If you forget to ring, the client will be delighted.
2. If we reduce our prices, we'll sell less.
3. If we don't leave now, we'll be early for our next appointment.
4. They may get a pay cut if sales go up this year.
5. If our sales go down, we might make a lot of money.
6. We may lose customers if our prices are very low.
7. You'll lose your job if you work hard.
8. If you get promoted, your salary won't go up.

Compare your answers with another pair.

2 In the sentences in Exercise 1, there are different constructions with *if*:

Example: *If* + present simple, *will/won't* + verb
(certain consequence)
If + present simple, *may (not) / might (not)* + verb
(possible consequence)

Now complete these sentences using the different constructions.

1. If I get home early tonight, ...
2. If there's nothing in the fridge at home this evening, ...
3. If I have some free time at the weekend, ...
4. If I can save some money this year, ...
5. If someone phones me after midnight tonight, ...

Interview a partner like this:

A: *What will you do if you get home early tonight?*
B: *I'll* ....
or
I may/might ....
or
I won't ....

3 Read this case study.

BILL JORDAN, the manager of a large DIY Superstore,★ is thinking about a change in his employment policy. He would like to increase the number of employees in their fifties and sixties to stock the shelves, work on the tills, and advise customers. He is 53 himself, and he believes that older members of staff are more helpful, more reliable and more knowledgeable.

Ron Catterick, the assistant manager, takes the opposite view. He would like to see more young people in their late teens and early twenties on the staff. He thinks that if they employ a lot of older people, the store will look very old-fashioned.

They are planning to discuss this subject at their next meeting.

★ DIY Superstore: a large shop where you can buy Do It Yourself products, e.g. paint, wallpaper, tools

What do you think? In groups, discuss what will happen if they employ more older people, and what will happen if they employ more younger people.

PERSONAL STUDY WORKBOOK

In your Personal Study Workbook, you will find more exercises to help you with your learning. For Unit 16, these include:

• exercises on conditional sentences, and the difference between *if* and *when*
• exercises on business vocabulary and the use of suffixes
• a text on future trends in our society (and an opportunity for you to predict future trends in your country)
• guidance on writing a business letter
• things to do with your speaking partner

REVIEW OF UNIT 14

1 Unwanted possessions   writing

We all have possessions that we haven't used very much. Write down at least three examples in sentences similar to these:

I've got some wine glasses that I've only used once.
I've got a pair of sunglasses that I've never worn.
I haven't used my phone card at all.

Compare your examples in groups.

2 Odd one out   vocabulary

Which is the 'odd one out' in each group, and why?

1. slippers   tracksuit   lounge   earrings
2. rabbit   horse   dog   parrot
3. rug   wardrobe   bedside table   desk
4. saxophone   flute   guitar   fur
5. lounge   hall   calculator   balcony
6. pets   skis   jewellery   toys

Discuss your answers with a partner.

REVIEW OF UNIT 15

1 Rules   speaking

What is a good rule? What is a bad rule? In groups, write a definition of a good rule and a bad rule, and then try to think of two good rules for your classroom and two bad rules.

Example: *If anyone is late for class they cannot come in. They have to wait for the next lesson.*
If anyone falls asleep, they have to take the group out for coffee.

Are these good rules or bad rules?

2 The good old days   had to, didn't have to, could(n't)

Complete these sentences in your own words. Then compare in small groups.

People who lived two hundred years ago …
– had to ....
– didn't have to ....
– could ....
– couldn't ....

People who lived two thousand years ago …
– had to ....
– didn't have to ....
– could ....
– couldn't ....

17

PICTURE THIS!

Language focus:
link words: *so that, otherwise*
sequencing: *first of all, secondly*
look + adj, *look like* + noun
could (be) for speculation
giving advice and warnings

Vocabulary:
photography
interiors of rooms

SAY CHEESE   link words: *so that, otherwise*

1 Have you got a camera? If *yes*, answer the questions below on the left. If *no*, answer the
questions on the right.

Yes	**No**
1. How long have you had your camera?	1. Have you ever owned a camera?
2. What kind is it?	2. If so, what kind was it?
3. How often do you use it?	3. Would you like to have one?
4. Are you particularly interested in photography?	4. Is there any special reason why you haven't got a camera?
5. What do you do with the pictures you take?	5. Do you like looking at other people's photos?
6. Do you think you'll buy another camera within the next two years?	6. Do you think you'll buy a camera within the next two years?

Find a partner who answered the other questions.
Ask the questions and listen to their answers.

2 Here is some advice on taking good photographs of *people*. Can you guess the meaning
of these words in the text while you read?

pose   avoid   squint   shadows   blurred

1. Get close to the person/people so that you only see the important details you want in the
picture.
2. Make the person/people feel relaxed. For example, talk to them, tell them jokes, or get
them to do something. When people just stand and *pose* for the camera they often look
unnatural and uncomfortable.
3. Choose the background carefully. *Avoid* backgrounds that are unpleasant or confusing. A
simple background is often best.
4. Make sure the lighting is correct. If the sun is in the person's eyes, they will *squint*. If the
sun is directly overhead, you may have lots of dark *shadows* under the person's nose and
chin.
5. When you take the picture make sure your hand doesn't move, otherwise the picture will
be *blurred*.
6. Take lots of pictures. All professionals know that you don't normally get a perfect picture
with just one photo.

Compare your answers with a partner.

3 Using the information in the text, choose the good pictures and the bad pictures from these examples. Work with a partner and then compare your answers with another pair. Make sure you can explain why the pictures are good or bad.

4 Can you remember the advice? Cover the text on the previous page and try to complete this text with suitable words and phrases.

First of all, get close to the person .... you only have the important information in the picture, and .... him/her .... relaxed. Secondly, choose the background carefully and .... backgrounds that are confusing or unpleasant. Thirdly, ... the lighting is correct. If the sun is in people's eyes, ... squint. If the sun is overhead, they may have lots of dark .... under their nose and chin. Fourthly, ... your hand doesn't move, ... the picture will be blurred. Finally, ... lots of photos.

5 Complete these sentences and compare them in groups.

1. I always carry my camera around with me so that ....
2. I carry my camera around my neck, otherwise ....
3. I sometimes use a zoom lens so that ....
4. I keep my camera in a case, otherwise ....
5. I keep my pictures in an album, otherwise ....

6 Match the following captions with the correct pictures above.

Me again, with a tree growing out of my head.
Is this a prison? No wonder I look depressed.

Now write your own captions for the other six photographs. Work on your own or with a partner.

1 The following advice is to a woman. What do you think she is going to do? Compare your answer with a partner.

First of all, try to find a good partner.
Secondly, don't forget to listen to the music.
Thirdly, try to avoid men who are shorter than you.
Finally, make sure you wear a comfortable pair of shoes.
And remember, if you make lots of mistakes, don't worry or panic.

2 Complete the sentences below with good advice for one of these people:

a. someone who is going to a second-hand car dealer to buy a second-hand car.
b. someone who is going up in an aeroplane and is frightened of flying.
c. someone who is babysitting for the first time.
d. someone who is going to a pet shop to buy a parrot.

First of all, try to ....
Secondly, don't forget to ....
Thirdly, try to avoid ....
Finally, make sure (that) ....
And remember, if .... , ...

3 Find a new partner. Tell them your suggestions. Do they think it is good advice?

4 ▭▭ ▭▭ Listen to someone giving advice about complaining in a shop. Do they think these things are a good idea or a bad idea?

– Take the receipt with you.   – Tell them you'll call the police if you don't get your money back.
– Make a lot of noise.   – Try to avoid a very busy time.
– Take someone else with you.   – Demand to see the manager.
– Be aggressive.

Compare your answers with a partner.

5 Discuss in small groups.

1. Do you agree with the speaker in Exercise 4?
2. What is the best way to complain in your country?
3. Have you got experience of complaining in shops?
4. Have you ever written a letter of complaint? Tell your group about it.

Unit 17 PICTURE THIS!

1 Look at the picture and complete the text. Underline the answer you think is best in each case.

The room in the picture looks like a (hall/reception area/living room). There is very little furniture, just two sofas facing each other, some armchairs at the end, and a table – it looks very (Italian/Scandinavian/British). There's a white object on the left which could be (a freezer/a piece of furniture/a piece of sculpture). The room itself looks very light, and (beautifully simple/rather bare/quite elegant). There is a woman sitting on one of the sofas who could be the (owner/receptionist/designer), and she's with a boy who is probably her son. They both look (quite relaxed/rather serious/very thoughtful).

Compare your answers with a partner.

2 Notice the use of these common phrases in the text:

look + adjective	e.g. *It looks Scandinavian.*
	They both look quite relaxed.
look like + noun	e.g. *It looks like a hall.*
could be + noun/adjective	e.g. *It could be a freezer.*
	She could be the owner.

Complete these sentences with your own ideas about the picture, then compare in groups.

.... looks ....
.... looks like ....
.... could be ....

3 ▭ Listen to someone who knows the room well talking about it. What facts do you learn? Make notes.

4 Work with a partner. Write a description of one of these rooms, including the phrases in Exercise 2. When you have finished you can find out more about the rooms on page 171.

1

2

PERSONAL STUDY WORKBOOK

In your Personal Study Workbook, you will find more exercises to help you with your learning. For Unit 17, these include:

- an exercise to practise *so that* and *otherwise*
- a vocabulary exercise on *make* and *do*, and other important verbs
- a poem about taking pictures
- writing an informal letter (giving instructions and advice)
- another page of your visual dictionary – at the beach, in town, in the country

---

REVIEW AND DEVELOPMENT

REVIEW OF UNIT 15

1 The story behind the photo   reading; articles

Sometimes the story behind a newspaper photo can be as interesting as the photo itself. Read the story of this photo and complete the gaps with *a/an*, *the*, or nothing.

This picture was taken by .... John Rogers, a newspaper photographer, during .... siege in .... embassy in .... London. A group of diplomats refused to leave .... building, and so armed police were positioned in .... office buildings near .... embassy. For four days and nights, Rogers and .... colleague hid in an empty office above the police. They were even given food through a letterbox. On the fifth day of .... siege, Rogers took this unusual photo. A secretary in one of .... buildings agreed to lend her office to the police if they watered her plants each morning. As you can see from .... photo, they did as they were told.

2 Different meanings of common verbs vocabulary

Translate these sentences into your own language and then, if possible, compare your answers with someone who speaks the same language.

1. I left home at seven o'clock.
2. I left school five years ago.
3. I left my homework on the bus.
4. I left my keys with the neighbour.
5. I broke my pencil.
6. I broke my leg.
7. I broke the world record.
8. I broke the rules.
9. I can see the church clearly.
10. I see him every week for an hour.
11. Yes, I see the problem.
12. I didn't see the accident.

There are three verbs in the sentences above. How many did you need in the sentences in your own language?

Can you think of another verb in English that can be translated in different ways in your language?

REVIEW OF UNIT 16

1 How well do you know your classmates? if sentences with will

Think about the next lesson and complete these sentences with the name of someone in the class. (It can also be the name of your teacher.)

Example: *If ..Anna... is late, no one will be surprised.*

1. If .... is late, no one will be surprised.
2. If .... doesn't come, it will be very unusual.
3. If someone forgets their book, it won't be ....
4. If .... answers a question, it will probably be correct.
5. If someone tells a joke, it will probably be ....
6. If .... asks a question, it will be surprising.
7. If someone makes a lot of noise, it won't be ....
8. If someone is too hot or cold, it will probably be ....

Compare your answers with a partner. Then write two or three sentences of your own, like the ones above, to tell the rest of the class.

2 Contractions and linking pronunciation

A ▭ Listen and complete the following sentences.

1. If he makes a noise, ...
2. If she does it again, ...
3. If they sit down, ...
4. If he comes, ...
5. If she smokes, ...
6. If they get on, ...
7. If he puts it on, ...
8. If they turn it on, ...

Compare your answers with a partner.

B ▭ Listen to the sentences again and notice:

– the contraction of *will*, e.g. *I'll, he'll, she'll.*
– the pronunciation of *him, her* and *them.*
– the way words are joined together, e.g. *shut up, take it off.*

Now practise with a partner, like this:

A: What'll you do if he makes a noise?
B: I'll tell him to shut up.

18

LISTS

<table>
<tr><td>Language focus:
requests, suggestions and
arrangements
telephoning</td><td>Vocabulary:
crime
common fixed phrases
verb + noun collocations
keeping a vocabulary notebook</td></tr>
</table>

WHO MAKES LISTS?   vocabulary

1 📖 Work in groups of three. Don't speak to each other.
Listen and follow the instructions.

2 Some people organise their lives by making lists. Do you write lists? Look at the following list and tick the ones that you make. Add your own at the bottom.

	often (✓✓)	occasionally (✓)	never (✗)
a shopping list	....	....	....
a list of holiday preparations	....	....	....
a list of people to invite to a party	....	....	....
a greetings card list	....	....	....
a list of things you have to do at work	....	....	....
a list of letters to write or phone calls to make	....	....	....
a list of jobs to do in the house	....	....	....
a list of problems to solve	....	....	....
a list of things you've bought and money spent	....	....	....
a list of places to visit	....	....	....
a list of things to do this week/month	....	....	....
a list of things to take to the dry cleaner	....	....	....
....	....	....	....
....	....	....	....

Compare your answers in groups.

3 Add up the number of ticks you have in Exercise 1 and organise yourselves into three groups:

Group A: those with a score of 0–6.
Group B: those with a score of 7–12.
Group C: those with a score above 12.

Do you agree with these statements? Discuss in your groups and then add two more you think are true.

People who write lists:
- are very organised.
- have a very bad memory.
- are very busy people.
- like organising things, and other people.
- worry too much.
- get things done.
- think that other people are lazy and should make lists.
- often don't do the things that are on their lists.

- ....
- ....

4 Spend ten minutes looking back through this book. Make a list of all the lists you can find.

Example: *A list of things you do in the classroom (page 40 Unit 6)*
          A list of things/places you find in a city centre (page 18 Unit 3)

Compare your lists in groups.

1 Many people learn vocabulary by writing vertical lists of words in a notebook. What do you do? Tell a partner and show them.

2 Now look at this list and use a dictionary to help you with new words if you don't understand German.

never mind	es macht nichts
crowd	eine Gruppe, eine Meute
escape	flüchten
at least	mindestens
catch	fangen, erwischen
among	zwischen
apart from	ausser
stomach	der Magen
beard	der Bart
I'm afraid not	leider nicht; Ich befürchte, nein
get away	flüchten
average	Durchschnitt
on foot	zu Fuss
punch	schlagen, boxen
on his/her own	alleine
smash	zerschlagen
recognize	erkennen
witness	ein Zeuge/eine Zeugin
height	die Höhe
I don't think so	Ich glaube nicht; Ich denke nicht
empty	leer

3 🔊 Listen to this advice from a teacher and make notes in the box.

1. Translations are good for some words, but an explanation is necessary for other words.
2. ....
3. ....
4. ....
5. ....

4 Take a new sheet of paper and reorganise the list of words in Exercise 2, including some of the ideas from the recording, and any ideas of your own. When you have finished, move round the class and compare your results. Do you think these ideas are useful?

5 Continue each of these dialogues and try to include as many words as possible from the list in Exercise 2.

POLICEMAN: Are you all right?
SHOPKEEPER: Yes. I think so.
POLICEMAN: Good. Can you tell me what happened, then?
SHOPKEEPER: Well, I was just closing the shop for lunch when …

INSPECTOR MAC: Well, did you catch him?
PC BRAITHWAITE: I'm afraid not, sir. He got away.
INSPECTOR MAC: What? He escaped! How?
PC BRAITHWAITE: …

Read your dialogues to another pair. Are they happy with the way you used all the words and phrases?

ORGANISATION

1 Organise the following things into three lists and give each one a title. Work on your own or with a partner.

borrow tapes from Jim
send fax to D.I.P.
get suntan lotion
tell the neighbours
write the agenda for Monday
arrange meeting with Mrs Howard
send out invitations
get my hair cut
buy a new pair of shorts

confirm the flight
finish report on Greece
leave keys with the neighbours
organise the catering
cancel Friday's meeting
hire 50 champagne glasses
see if Mary can feed Felix
buy a new corkscrew
check delivery schedules for July

Compare your answers in groups.

2 With a partner, add two more possible things for each list and then compare them with another pair.

3 Imagine you have to do the following things from the three lists.

   – phone Mary at home (Can she feed your cat, Felix?)
   – phone shop (Is it possible to hire champagne glasses?)
   – phone Mrs Howard (to arrange a meeting).

Work with a partner. Choose one of these things and then decide which of the following sentences and phrases you will probably need in your telephone conversation.

– Hi, is that ......?	– How about next Thursday?
– I wonder if you could help me?	– That's very kind of you. Thanks.
– Could I speak to ......?	– I'm fine, thanks. And you?
– while I'm away	– When could I pick them up?
– Do I have to leave a deposit?	– No, I'm afraid I have to go to Paris.
– Is that convenient for you?	– Would it be possible for you to ......?

4 ▭ Listen to the conversation you chose on the recording.
Did they use the same phrases as you? Did they use any others in the list that you did not include?

Check your answers in Tapescript 10 on page 174.

5 With your partner, make up another conversation similar to the ones you listened to in Exercise 4. This time, change the reason for phoning, but try to include phrases from the list in Exercise 3.

PERSONAL STUDY WORKBOOK

In your Personal Study Workbook, you will find more exercises to help you with your learning. For Unit 18, these include:

• exercises on social English – telephoning, apologising, and making arrangements
• vocabulary exercises on different topics
• a reading passage about how we remember things
• a pronunciation exercise on intonation
• activities to do with your speaking partner
• another page of your visual dictionary – lexical sets

REVIEW AND DEVELOPMENT

REVIEW OF UNIT 16

1 Do you know the difference?   if or when?

Complete the sentences with *if* or *when*.

1. I'll give you a ring .... I get home.
2. .... anyone wants me, tell them I'm in the accounts department.
3. .... I'm 50, I probably won't have much hair left.
4. .... I win the competition, I'll be a bit surprised, but very pleased.
5. .... it rains tomorrow, we'll have to stay at home.
6. The teacher can help you .... we have our break.
7. .... there is enough time, we'll stop for something to eat.
8. .... my listening is a bit better, I'll be able to watch films in English and understand them.

2 What will people think? $\boxed{\textit{will and might}}$

Make up some generalisations about social
behaviour in your country. Complete the
sentences below using one of the suggested
endings in the box, or write your own.

$$\text{people} \begin{array}{l} \text{will} \\ \text{might} \end{array} \text{think it's} \left\{ \begin{array}{l} \text{normal.} \\ \text{strange.} \\ \text{surprising.} \\ \text{silly.} \\ \text{rude.} \\ \text{shocking.} \end{array} \right.$$

In my country, if you …
- ask permission to leave the room in a meeting, …
- don't wait your turn in a shop, …
- pay the amount on a price tag in a market, …
- stand up and give a young child a seat on a crowded train, …
- shake hands with the people you work with every morning, …
- call your boss by their surname, …
- wear evening dress to go to a wedding reception, …
- sneeze in public and don't apologise, …
- don't sit at a table to eat your dinner, …

REVIEW OF UNIT 17

1 An intelligent guess $\boxed{\textit{looks/looks like/could be}}$

Write sentences about the
people and places in the picture,
using these structures:

Examples:

The man on the right …
- *could be on holiday.*
- *looks like a fish.*
- *looks a bit strange.*

Discuss your sentences in groups.

2 Don't forget to take a dictionary $\boxed{\textit{giving advice}}$

Complete the sentences with advice for a friend who is going to study English in an
English-speaking country.

Try to ....

Make sure you ....

Try to avoid ....

Don't forget to ....

If ...., ...

19

PUT YOUR TRUST IN OTHERS

Language focus:	Vocabulary:
if sentences with *will* and *would*	adjectives ending *-ed* and *-ing*
offers and requests	describing speech acts, e.g. agree, complain
	guessing words in context

APPEARANCES CAN BE DECEPTIVE   guessing from context; *-ed* and *-ing* adjectives

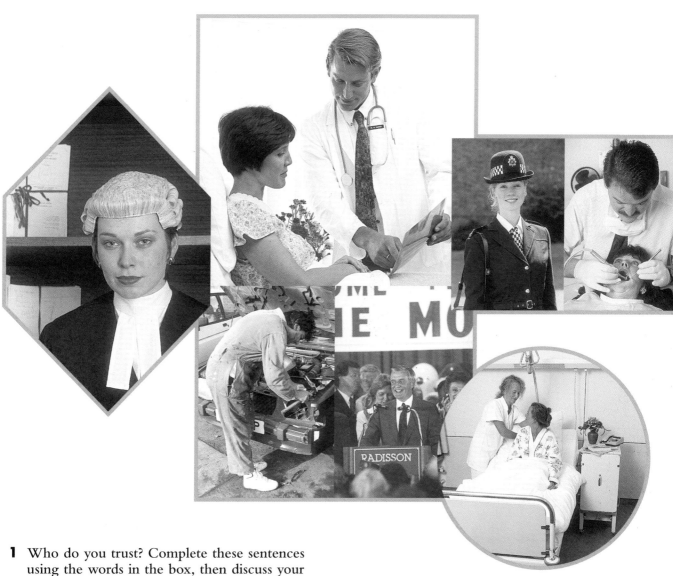

1 Who do you trust? Complete these sentences using the words in the box, then discuss your answers in groups.

I always trust ....

I trust .... most of the time.

I trust .... some of the time.

I don't trust .... very much.

I don't trust .... at all.

dentists	doctors
lawyers	car mechanics
politicians	nurses
the police	myself

2 Read this story about the dangers of trust and put the sentences in the correct order.

a. At that point she realised the *hitchhiker* was a man. She stopped the car. 'I can't see out of the *rear* window,' she said. 'Would you mind clearing it for me?' The hitchhiker *nodded* and opened the door.

1 b. A *nun* was driving through lonely *countryside*; it was getting dark and it was raining.

c. 'I can't leave her out in this weather,' the nun said to herself. So, she stopped the car and opened the door.

d. When she reached the next village she stopped. She noticed the hitchhiker had left a handbag behind, so she picked it up and opened it.

e. Suddenly she saw an old woman by the side of the road. She was holding out her hand as if she wanted a lift.

f. '*Nasty* weather,' she said. Again the old woman nodded. No matter what the nun asked her, the old woman gave no answer except for a nod. Then the nun noticed the woman's hands which were large and hairy.

g. 'Do you want a lift?' she asked. The old woman nodded and climbed into the car.

h. She gave a *gasp*. Inside the bag was a gun.

i. As soon as the hitchhiker was out of the car, the terrified nun drove off.

j. After *a while* the nun said, 'Have you been waiting long?' The old woman shook her head. 'Very *odd*,' thought the nun. She tried again.

Compare your answers with a partner.

3 Sometimes it is possible to guess the exact meaning of a new word from the context; sometimes it is possible to guess the general meaning; and sometimes it is very difficult to guess the meaning.

Examples: 1. *It was raining very hard and I got soaked.* (*soaked* here probably means *wet* or *very wet*.)
2. *He was a kind, gentle, tolerant man, and everyone liked him.* (*tolerant* is clearly a positive word here but there are too many possibilities for us to guess the exact meaning.)
3. *When the boys passed by, several were whistling and one had a big stick.* (from this context alone it is almost impossible to guess the meaning of *whistling* or *stick*.)

If they are new, try to guess the meaning of these words as they appeared in the story. Are they easy to guess or difficult to guess? Discuss in groups.

a nun	a hitchhiker	rear	countryside
a while	nasty	to nod	a gasp	odd

4 At one point in the story the nun was *terrifíed* because the situation was *terrifýing*. So, how do you feel:

– when the weather is very depressing?
– in an embarrassing situation?
– during a frightening experience?
– when your work is disappointing?
– when something is boring?

Now think of examples about yourself to complete these sentences, and then compare them in groups.

Example: *I get bored* ...when I have nothing to do.........

1. I get bored ....
2. I get embarrassed ....
3. I'm shocked by ....
4. I'm fascinated by ....
5. I get frightened ....

NEW NEIGHBOURS   *if* sentences with *would* and *might*

1 Imagine this man and his young child moved into your street or building. What would you do if he did any of the things below in the first week?

If he invited me to his new home for a drink,
If he asked me for some sugar,
If he wanted to borrow a hammer,
If he made a lot of noise at night,
If he asked me to babysit for half an hour,
If he wanted to look round my home,
If he wanted to borrow my car,
If he gave me a bottle of champagne,
If he told me he was Dustin Hoffman's cousin,
If he offered me a lift to work,

I'd
(I would) { accept (it).
agree (to …).
complain.
refuse. }

I wouldn't { believe him.
give him one.
lend him some. }

I would ignore it.

Tell the class what you would do.

2 Look at the sentences again and answer these questions:

1. What tense is used after *if* in each sentence?
2. Are the sentences about the past or the present/future?
3. What construction is used in the second part of each sentence?
4. Are the sentences about a real situation or an imaginary one?

Now look at these *if* sentences. How are they different in *form* and *meaning* from the sentences in Exercise 1? Discuss with a partner.

If I work hard, my English will improve.
If you take these tablets, they will help your migraine.

3 Underline the correct answers in these sentences.

1. If I (see/saw) him tomorrow, (I'll/I'd) give him the book.
2. (I'll/I'd) be very surprised if a stranger (gives/gave) me some money in the street for no reason.
3. If I (break/broke) both my legs tomorrow, (I'll/I might) write a book.
4. If I (get/got) home on time this afternoon, (I'll/I'd) phone you.
5. (I'll/I'd) apply for that job in Oslo if I (know/knew) how to speak Norwegian.
6. If I (have/had) a lot of money now, (I'll/I would) give up work.
7. If they (don't/didn't) come soon, (we'll/we'd) never catch that bus.
8. If I (am/were) you, (I'll/I'd) definitely accept that new job.

4 Complete these sentences about the man in the picture, and then add two more of your own.

If he used my parking space, I ....

If he wanted to use my phone, I ....

I'd complain if he ....

I might refuse if he ....

....

....

Discuss your sentences with a partner.

5 Now think about a real situation. What do you do when new people move into the flat/house next to you, or when you move into a new flat/house? Do you introduce yourself to your neighbours? Do you invite them into your home? Discuss in groups.

IT'S UP TO YOU   offers and requests

1 Divide the class in half. One half, in small groups, should read and discuss these situations. The rest of the class should read and discuss the situations on page 172.

1. This man knocks on your door and tells you that he lived in your home when he was a boy and he would like to see how it has changed. Would you believe him? Would you let him in?

2. This woman stops you in the street and tells you she has left her purse at home and hasn't got any money for her bus fare. Would you believe her? Would you give her any money?

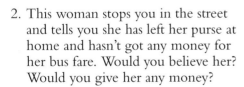

3. This man, seeing you walking in the rain, stops and offers you a lift. Would you accept? What would you say?

4. This woman is standing outside the front door of a flat. She tells you that she has left her key inside. She wants you to help her break a window to get in. Would you help her? What would you say?

5. This man offers you a hundred dollars for no reason. He tells you that he is rich and doesn't need the money. What would your reaction be? What would you say?

2 Find someone who discussed the other situations. Tell them your answer to the first situation, then look at each other's picture. Continue for all five situations.

3 🔲 Listen to the recording. The first woman, Joumana, is talking about the situations on page 172, and the second woman, Lorelei, about the situations on pages 123 and 124. What would they do in each case?

	Joumana	Lorelei
Situation 1	....	....
Situation 2	....	....
Situation 3	....	....
Situation 4	....	....
Situation 5	....	....

4 In small groups, imagine what the people actually said in the above situations:

Example: Situation 1.
> *'I'm sorry to bother you, but I grew up in this house.*
> *Could I possibly have a look inside to see how it has changed?'*

5 With a partner, choose one of the situations and improvise the complete conversation.
When you are ready, act it out for the others in the class.

PERSONAL STUDY WORKBOOK

In your Personal Study Workbook, you will find more exercises to help you with
your learning. For Unit 19, these include:

- exercises to practise conditionals
- another story about the dangers of trust, and an exercise on contextual guesswork
- vocabulary exercises on adjectives ending -*ing* and -*ed*, and word building
- a dictation
- another speaking partners activity

REVIEW AND DEVELOPMENT

REVIEW OF UNIT 17

1 Strange comparisons   `looks like a ...`

A Complete the questions using the words in the box.

| a dog | a painting | a bird | a statue | a museum | an adult |
| a person's face | a fruit basket | a gun | | | |

Have you ever seen

a man who looks like ..*a dog*......?

a woman who looks like ....?

a photo that looks like ....?

a house that looks like ....?

a vegetable that looks like ....?

a telephone that looks like ....?

a hat that looks like ....?

a cigarette lighter that looks like ....?

a child who looks like ....?

A sofa that looks like ...

B 📼 Listen to the recording. Did you complete the questions in the same way as the speakers?

Listen again and make notes on their answers. Then compare in groups.

C Now ask and answer the questions you wrote in groups.

2 Opposites   vocabulary

Many of these words appeared in Unit 17. Find ten pairs of opposites.

remember	both	background	nice	simple	tense	second-hand
panic	unpleasant	town	relaxed	complicated	stay calm	forget
countryside	neither	new	clear	foreground	confusing	

With a partner, practise the opposites in dialogues, like this:

A: *Did she panic?*
B: *No, she stayed very calm.*
A: *Is the man standing in the background?*
B: *No, he's in the foreground.*

REVIEW OF UNIT 18

1 Situations   social English

Write down your answers for these situations.

1. You telephone a colleague to cancel an appointment. What do you say?
2. You arrive late for class. What do you say?
3. You ask someone for help, but they are busy. What do you say?
4. Your friend invites you for dinner and asks you when you want to come. Make a suggestion.
5. Your car won't start, and you need it urgently. You telephone the garage and ask them to come and repair it. What do you say to them?
6. You can't find the street you want, so you go into a shop for help. What are your first words?

Discuss your answers in groups.

2 Six things you can cancel   vocabulary: collocation

Complete the following lists on your own.

6 things you can cancel: Example: *a flight*

5 things you can arrange:

4 things you can hire:

3 things to check before leaving the house:

2 things you can confirm in advance:

1 thing you can solve:

Compare your lists with others in the class.

3 Sounds and spelling   pronunciation

Look at the underlined letters in these words, and find a word in Box A with the same sound as a word in Box B.

Example: Gr<u>ee</u>ce   at l<u>ea</u>st

A

am<u>o</u>ng	b<u>o</u>rrow	aver<u>a</u>ge	n<u>ou</u>n
h<u>ei</u>ght	Gr<u>ee</u>ce	<u>ow</u>n	champ<u>a</u>gne
s<u>o</u>lution	c<u>o</u>rkscrew		

B

b<u>u</u>sy	sh<u>o</u>pping	at l<u>ea</u>st	<u>o</u>rganise
n<u>o</u>tebook	n<u>ei</u>ghbour	cr<u>ow</u>d	
st<u>o</u>mach	cr<u>i</u>me	<u>a</u>rrange	

⊡ Listen to the recording to check your answers.

20

THE SENSES

Language focus:
so do I / neither do I
will/might/won't for predictions
it sounds/smells/tastes like ...
I like the smell/taste/feel of ...

Vocabulary:
likes and dislikes
materials, food, nationalities,
technology

1 The five senses in English are taste, touch, smell, sight and hearing.
Which professions depend on particular senses?

Examples: *A painter depends on his or her sight.*
A doctor needs a good sense of touch.
A coffee importer needs a good sense of smell and taste.

In small groups, make as many examples as possible.

2 Look up any new words, then complete the questionnaire on your own.

For each group of words, mark the things you like (✓) and the things you don't like (✗).

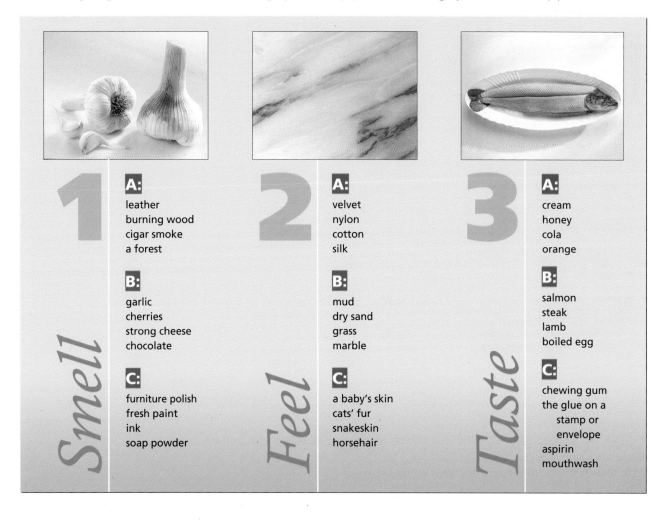

1 Smell

A:
leather
burning wood
cigar smoke
a forest

B:
garlic
cherries
strong cheese
chocolate

C:
furniture polish
fresh paint
ink
soap powder

2 Feel

A:
velvet
nylon
cotton
silk

B:
mud
dry sand
grass
marble

C:
a baby's skin
cats' fur
snakeskin
horsehair

3 Taste

A:
cream
honey
cola
orange

B:
salmon
steak
lamb
boiled egg

C:
chewing gum
the glue on a
  stamp or
  envelope
aspirin
mouthwash

3 Work with a partner. Listen to their opinions, and say if yours is the same or different, like this:

Same opinion

A: I like the smell of cigar smoke.
B: **So** do I.
(*two positive sentences*)

A: I don't like the feel of velvet.
B: **Neither** do I.
(*two negative sentences*)

Different opinion

A: I love the smell of fresh paint.
B: Oh, I don't. I hate it!

A: I don't like the taste of honey.
B: Oh, I do – it's wonderful!

For a more detailed explanation of the grammar of this point see pages 168 and 169.

4 Read the text and complete the table on the next page, with specific examples for different countries.

Smells around the world

● Banana is the favourite smell of most people around the world. It beats peppermint, lemon and vanilla by a short head, according to a sixteen-country study. The least favourite smell is natural gas – even more disliked than the smell of skunk.*

● The University of California conducted a study in which 22 smells were tested on volunteers from different countries. The results showed some interesting regional variations.

● The English, who don't drink root beer, like the smell very much, almost as much as anise,* which they don't drink much of either. The French favourite is anise, but they find garlic unpleasant, and worse than smoke or skunk.

● The Poles love the smell of pickle,* which they rate as second only to banana and cherry. They also like the smell of pizza, as do the Swiss. Surprisingly, the Swiss don't like the healthy smell of oil

of wintergreen,* but it is extremely popular in California. The English and Poles, however, don't like it either.

● For the Norwegians and Swedes, lemon is the favourite. The English find it best for cleaning products, but the Germans find it disgusting.

● The Finns are much less enthusiastic about chocolate and pickle than their Scandinavian neighbours.

Glossary
* skunk: small black and white animal which makes a smell when attacked or afraid
* anise: French alcoholic drink
* pickle: vegetables preserved in vinegar and spices
* oil of wintergreen: a product used by athletes for aches and pains

	Likes	*Dislikes*
English	....	....
Poles	....	....
French	....	....
Swiss	....	....
Americans (Californians)	....	....
Germans	....	....
Norwegians and Swedes	....	....

5 What smells do people from your country like and dislike, do you think? Discuss in groups.

SOUNDS OF THE TWENTIETH CENTURY
will/might/won't

1 ⊂⊃ Listen to the recording, and write down what you can hear.

Example: 1. *It sounds like someone opening a can of fizzy drink.*
or
I think it's someone opening a can of fizzy drink.

2. ....
3. ....
4. ....
5. ....
6. ....
7. ....
8. ....
9. ....

Compare your answers with a partner.

2 Which of these sounds are:

– quite pleasant?   – important?
– irritating?   – useful?

Discuss in groups and give reasons for your answers.

3 ⊂⊃ Work with a partner. Choose one of the sounds and build a short dialogue round it. First listen to the example on the recording.

Act out your dialogue for others in the class.

SENSORY PREFERENCES

129

4 Imagine the world in fifty years' time. In groups, predict which objects will still be common. Use these expressions:

Example: ***I think we'll still*** *have drinks in cans.*
or
I think we might still *have drinks in cans.*
or
I don't think we'll *have drinks in cans.*
or
I'm sure we won't *have drinks in cans.*

5 Work in small groups. Choose two or three of the objects which we won't have, and decide what will replace them.

Example: *Instead of doorbells, visitors will speak into a microphone.*

Compare your ideas with the rest of the class.

CHOOSING PERFUMES AND EAU DE COLOGNE
sense verbs

1 Bring some perfume, eau de cologne or after-shave to class. Let other people smell it and say what they think.

Examples: *This smells lovely.*
very sweet.
a bit strong.
of lemon/honey, etc.

2 Answer these questions and then compare in groups.

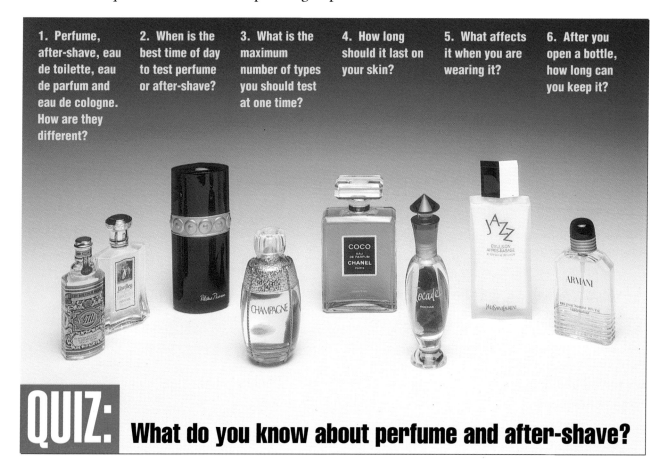

1. Perfume, after-shave, eau de toilette, eau de parfum and eau de cologne. How are they different?

2. When is the best time of day to test perfume or after-shave?

3. What is the maximum number of types you should test at one time?

4. How long should it last on your skin?

5. What affects it when you are wearing it?

6. After you open a bottle, how long can you keep it?

QUIZ: What do you know about perfume and after-shave?

3 🔲🔲 Now find out the answers. Listen to the recording and make notes. Compare with a partner.

4 Work in groups of three or four. Write a short questionnaire (4–5 questions) to find out about the use of perfumes or after-shave in your class.

Example: *How often do you buy perfume, eau de cologne or after-shave?*

Give your questionnaire to another group to complete.

PERSONAL STUDY WORKBOOK

In your Personal Study Workbook, you will find more exercises to help you with your learning. For Unit 20, these include:

- an exercise to practise *so* and *neither*
- a vocabulary exercise on compound words
- another listen and answer exercise to practise listening and revise vocabulary
- a pronunciation exercise on sounds and spelling
- listening to part of a story and writing part of it yourself
- another page of your visual dictionary – revision

REVIEW AND DEVELOPMENT

REVIEW OF UNIT 18

1 Listen and answer   vocabulary

🔲 Listen and write down your answers.

Compare your answers with a partner, and then check them together using Tapescript 11 on page 174.

Then tell your partner to shut their book. Ask them the questions and see how quickly they can answer.

2 On the telephone   speaking

With a partner, practise these situations. Do each one twice so you can change roles.

1. Imagine your partner is your best friend. You want to arrange an evening out, e.g. in a bar or restaurant. Phone your friend, find out if they are free this evening or tomorrow evening, and make the arrangements.
2. Your partner works for the same company as you but you don't know them. Phone your partner and arrange a business meeting for a convenient time this week or next week.
3. Your partner is the receptionist at a hotel. Phone the hotel and book a double room for next weekend.

3 Lexical sets   vocabulary

Add two more things to each list, and then compare your lists in groups.

a. bed; wardrobe; mirror; ....
b. catch; witness; get away; ....
c. cheque; credit card; deposit; ....

---

d. organise; meeting; agenda; ....

e. suitcase; shorts; suntan lotion; ....

REVIEW OF UNIT 19

1 Adjectives describing emotions   vocabulary

Match the adjectives with the pictures.

delighted   astonished   upset   nervous   aggressive   terrified

2 How would you feel?   if sentences with *would* or *might*

Complete the sentences about yourself.

Example: *I think I would be very nervous if I appeared on TV.*

1. I think I would be very nervous if ....

2. I would be absolutely astonished if ....

3. I might become aggressive if ....

4. I would be delighted if ....

5. I would be very upset if ....

6. I might be terrified if ....

Move around the class and tell others what you wrote.

21

TIME

Language focus:	Vocabulary:
used to + verb	time expressions
tense revision	ordinal numbers
time clauses	
common errors	

A NEW WORLD CALENDAR

dates/ordinal numbers; time expressions

1 You almost certainly know the months of the year and dates in English. But which are difficult to *pronounce*? Work with a partner, saying the words, and circle any which you think are more difficult.

January	July
February	August
March	September
April	October
May	November
June	December

1st	9th	17th	25th
2nd	10th	18th	26th
3rd	11th	19th	27th
4th	12th	20th	28th
5th	13th	21st	29th
6th	14th	22nd	30th
7th	15th	23rd	31st
8th	16th	24th	

Listen to the recording to check your pronunciation.

2 Practise dates like this: the seventeenth of July   the twenty-first of October

Find out everyone's birthday. Stop asking when you can remember them all.

3 Work with a partner. How quickly can you answer these questions? Don't use a diary!

1. What is the date today?
2. How many days are there in April, October, February and March?
3. What is the extra date in a leap year?
4. If today is May 27th, what day of the week is June 2nd?
5. You agree to meet someone next month on the fifteenth. What day is that?
6. You also agree to meet someone on Tuesday week (the Tuesday after next Tuesday). What date is that?

4 Did that take quite a long time? If so, you may be interested in this text. Read it and answer the questions.

Leapday? What's that?

Why is our calendar so complicated? Why should it be so difficult to work out whether the 15th is a Tuesday or a Thursday? Or whether next Wednesday is the 10th or the 11th? Jurek Biegus believes these problems are unnecessary and he has proposed a simple solution.

We could divide the year into 13 months, with each month having 28 days, and with each month starting on the same day. Therefore, the 1st, 8th, 15th, and 22nd day of each month would be a Monday; the 2nd, 9th, 16th, and 23rd would be a Tuesday; and so on. This means that people would automatically know what day the 26th falls on, and they would automatically know that the second Friday in the month is the 12th.

There are still two problems. Firstly, 13 months with 28 days is 364 days. What happens to the missing day? Jurek Biegus proposes that the day after December 28th should be New Year's Day, and then the next day becomes January 1st. Secondly, what about leap years? Biegus suggests that every fourth year, the day between Sunday 28th February and Monday 1st March is called 'Leapday'. Simple.

All that remains, says Biegus, is to find a name for the thirteenth month.

True or false?

1. Biegus would like to divide the year into 13 months.
2. Each month would last for 28 days.
3. Each month would begin on a Sunday.
4. A calendar year would now become only 364 days.
5. New Year's Day would not have a date.
6. Every year, the day after 28th February would be called 'Leapday'.

5 Using this new calendar, think of positive consequences, negative consequences, and interesting consequences. Work in groups.

For example, how would it affect:
– people's birthdays?
– businesses/companies?
– the seasons of the year?
– the manufacture and sales of diaries and calendars?
– the period between Christmas and New Year?
– astrology?
– the superstition of Friday (or Tuesday) the 13th (or 17th) in some countries?
– the manufacture of clocks, watches and computers?
– your country's national holidays?

Can you think of any other consequences, and a name for the thirteenth month? Discuss in groups.

1 Work with a partner and put these time expressions in order from the past to the future.

> the day before yesterday   in five days' time   in the 19th century
> next year   a couple of years ago   the day after tomorrow   right now
> the week after next   tonight   a fortnight ago   last week

Now put the correct date next to each expression. (If it is a period of time, put the date of the beginning of the period.)

2 Look at the three pictures and decide who said these things. Give reasons for your decision.

1. When I was a child I used to play with my computer a lot.
2. I used to have a lot of problems with my children, but things are better now.
3. When I was younger I used to have long hair.
4. I used to play a lot of tennis, but I'm too old now.
5. I used to work every weekend when I had my own business, but not any more.
6. I used to have fights with my sister, but now we get on OK.
7. I used to love punk music.
8. I never used to read much, but these days I really enjoy it.

Compare your answers in small groups.

Jack

Val

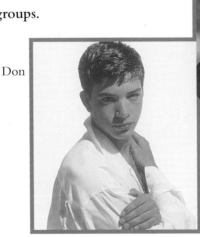

Don

3 If you *used to do* something, it means you did it regularly or it was true for a period of time in the past, but now things are different. How could you complete these sentences?

I used to play with my computer a lot, but ....

When I was younger I used to have long hair, but ....

I used to love punk music, but ....

4 ▭ Listen to the three people in Exercise 2 talking about themselves. Which sentences go with which speaker? Write the sentence numbers next to the names.

Jack ....   Val ....   Don ....

Compare your answers with a partner.

Were some of your guesses in Exercise 2 wrong? If so, why?

5 Time passes, and our lives, tastes and interests change. Look back at your past: what changes can you see? Complete these sentences, then discuss them in groups.

Example: DRINKS: *I used to hate* .. the taste of tonic water, but I quite like it now ....

CLOTHES: I used to wear ....

FOOD: I never used to like .... but now

....

MUSIC: I used to listen to .... but these days

....

HAIR: I used to have ....

ACTIVITIES: I never used to enjoy .... but now

....

BELIEFS: I used to think ....

Think of other ways in which your life has changed in the last ten years. Tell your group.

1 Work in groups of three or four. You need some counters and dice. Your teacher will explain the game.

2 Your teacher will give you a copy of all the sentences from the game you have just played. With a partner, correct all the mistakes, and keep the sheet as a record of the game.

PERSONAL STUDY WORKBOOK

In your Personal Study Workbook, you will find more exercises to help you with your learning. For Unit 21, these include:

- a chance to test your ability with numbers
- an exercise to practise *used to do*
- more practice with selected vocabulary and time expressions
- a text describing another way to organise our time
- poems about time
- practice in writing messages

REVIEW AND DEVELOPMENT

REVIEW OF UNIT 19

1 Imagine ... | *if* sentences with *would*; vocabulary |

Complete the questionnaire. If you are not happy with (a), (b) and (c), write your own answer beside (d).

1. Imagine your school offered you a free place in a class for one month. Would you:
   a. accept?
   b. refuse?
   c. not believe it?
   d. ....

2. Imagine your partner (as usual) forgot to bring their course book. Would you:
   a. lend them your book?
   b. give them your book?
   c. tell them to bring their book next time?
   d. ....

3. Imagine the director of your school asked you to make a ten-minute speech in English at a school party. Would you:
   a. agree immediately?
   b. refuse immediately?
   c. say you wanted to think about it?
   d. ....

4. Imagine your teacher was very lonely and didn't know anyone in town. Would you:
   a. invite them for a coffee after class?
   b. invite them to your home?
   c. ignore them?
   d. ....

5. Imagine your teacher asked you to help another person in class who couldn't understand an exercise. Would you:
   a. agree to help?
   b. make an excuse?
   c. refuse?
   d. ....

6. Imagine that your partner suddenly felt ill in the middle of a lesson. Would you:
   a. offer to take them outside?
   b. tell the teacher?
   c. ignore them?
   d. ....

Compare your answers in groups.

Work with a partner. Write one more question with three possible answers, and ask at least three other people to answer it.

REVIEW OF UNIT 20

1 Glass feels like marble vocabulary

Using words from each column, try to make twelve sentences in two minutes.

Example: *Glass feels like marble.*

glass			a typewriter
a doorbell			wild flowers
sugar			dirty socks
yoghurt			Swedish
Norwegian			fine sand
some perfume	sounds		sour cream
soap powder	tastes		pepper
chilli	looks	like	wood
some cheese	feels		marble
a small horse	smells		an alarm
some plastic			a donkey
a computer keyboard			honey
garlic			velvet
soft fur			onion

Compare your sentences with a partner.

Now make some sentences of your own. Tell a partner.

Examples: *My brother looks like a film star.*
            My cooking tastes like dog food.

2 We seem to agree so do I / neither can I; stress and intonation

A Work with a partner. Listen to the recording. One of you write down what the man (Bob) says, the other write down what the woman (Rebecca) says.

Compare the two parts of the dialogue. How often does Rebecca agree with Bob?

B Rebecca sounds friendly and interested, because of her tone and intonation.

Example: *I like the smell of lemons.   Mmmm, so do I.*

        I can speak Swedish.   So can I.

Work with a partner. Listen again, and try to imitate Rebecca's intonation. (It may sound funny to you, but it is natural in English!)

C Complete the sentence endings below yourself. Then work with a partner. Agree or disagree with each other, using appropriate intonation. Use the following structures:

So Neither	do can am	I.	Oh, really? I	do/don't. can/can't. am/'m not.

1. I'm ....
2. I'm not ....
3. I like ....
4. I speak ....
5. I don't like ....
6. I can ....
7. I live in ....
8. I can't ....

22

A SENSE OF HISTORY

> Language focus:
> past simple passive
> relative clauses: *who/which*
> link words: *although/however*
> remember + *-ing*
>
> Vocabulary:
> historical event verbs

HISTORICAL EVENTS

past simple passive; vocabulary

1 With a partner, look up any new verbs in the box, and then complete the sentences using the verbs, and the dates on the right.

invent	
die	
win	
elect	
kill	
murder	
assassinate	
resign	
become	
destroy	

1. General Franco of Spain .... in 1975.
2. President Nixon .... because of the Watergate scandal in ....
3. An earthquake in Armenia .... 45,000 people in 1988.
4. Fire .... part of Windsor Castle in 1992.
5. Carl Lewis .... the 100 metres gold medal in Seoul in ....
6. Theodore Maiman .... lasers in 1960.
7. The Russian people .... Boris Yeltsin as President of Russia in ....
8. India .... an independent country in ....
9. Anwar Sadat was .... in Egypt in ....
10. John Lennon was .... in 1980.

1947

1991

1981

1974

1988

CD Listen and check your answers.

2 CD Can you answer these questions? If not, listen to the recording again.

1. How long was General Franco ruler of Spain?
2. What is Windsor Castle, and what is the estimated cost of the damage?
3. Why did Carl Lewis finish second but still win the gold medal in Seoul?
4. Who killed Anwar Sadat?
5. Who shot John Lennon?

HISTORICAL EVENTS

3 Look at these sentences from Exercise 1 again. What is the difference between a and b, and can you see a reason for this difference? Discuss with a partner.

a. General Franco died in 1975.   b. John Lennon was murdered in 1980.
   President Nixon resigned in 1974.   Anwar Sadat was assassinated in 1981.

Check your answers in the Grammar Reference on page 169.

4 Look at the other sentences in Exercise 1, and change them from active to passive if you think it is possible. Check your answers with a partner.

5 The decision to use the active or passive will often depend on the focus of the sentence:

My car was stolen.
(We are interested in *the fact that my car was stolen* not who stole it.)

My friend's brother stole my car.
(We are interested in the fact that it was *my friend's brother* who stole my car.)

Work with a partner. Change the focus of these sentences and say more about the other person.

Examples: *The actor was arrested outside the theatre.*
            Twelve policemen arrested the actor outside the theatre.

            The drug was invented to help cancer patients.
            Professor Smith invented the drug to help cancer patients.

1. She was given antibiotics when she arrived.
   ....

2. The politician was assassinated when he began his speech.
   ....

3. The plane was hijacked on the way to Berlin.
   ....

4. The player was sent off for fighting.
   ....

5. The play was written for television.
   ....

6. The money was delivered to the wrong address.
   ....

1 How good is your memory? With a partner, read these sentences and decide if they are true or not.

1. The fire which destroyed Windsor Castle happened in 1992.
2. The man who invented lasers was called Maiman.
3. The scandal which destroyed Richard Nixon was called 'Waterfall'.
4. The man who won the Russian presidency in 1991 was Mikhail Gorbachev.
5. The gold medal which was won by Carl Lewis in Seoul was for the 1000 metres.

Look at the sentences again. When do we use *who* and when do we use *which*?

Which word would you use after the following?

Example: *the boy* .who.....

the woman ....   the country ....   the accident ....   the book ....
the Prime Minister ....   the people ....   the murder ....

Choose two of these and complete the sentences.

2 🔲🔲 Listen to four people talking about history lessons at school. Make notes on what each person learnt.

3 What can you remember about your history lessons at school? Use these phrases to discuss your memories in groups.

I remember studying …   *I remember our teacher telling us about …*
I remember seeing pictures of …   *I don't remember learning anything about …*
I remember seeing films about …   *The period of history which I liked most was …*

4 Sometimes children's understanding of history is not very clear. Before you read the text, look up these words in a dictionary.

to inhabit   an arrow   mummy (not mother)
to be hanged   wooden   navy

5 Now read the text. Which sentences are complete nonsense, and which sentences can you correct?

Strange ways kids rewrite history

The history that children write about in exams is sometimes a bit different from what their teachers taught them. And often the results are very funny indeed! Here are some examples from American children's junior high school and college essays. Can you spot the mistakes?

▼ Karl Marx became one of the Marx Brothers.
▼ Ancient Egypt was inhabited by Mummies who lived in the Sarah desert and wrote in hydraulics.
▼ William Tell shot an arrow through an apple while standing on his son's head.
▼ The Magna Carta stated that no man could be hanged twice for the same crime.
▼ The climate in the Sahara desert was so bad that the inhabitants had to live somewhere else.
▼ Abraham Lincoln was born in a wooden house which he built with his own hands.
▼ Queen Elizabeth's navy fought against the Spanish Armadillo.
▼ The American colonists won the war and no longer had to pay for taxis.

Compare your answers in groups.

1 Work in groups of three. Each of you should read a different story, make sure you understand it, and then shut your book and tell it to the rest of the group.

Bombs

In the 1940s, the Americans developed a new type of bomb. Millions of bats were caught and a small bomb was tied to each one. The plan was to release the bats over enemy cities, and when they landed on the roofs of buildings they would explode. Although the government spent $2 million on this new bomb, it was never used. However, on one occasion some bats escaped by accident and destroyed a general's car and an aircraft hangar.

No hair!

During the reign of Louis XIV of France, a mysterious illness swept through Europe. Nobody knew the cause, but one of the effects was that people's hair fell out. Louis himself had the illness and his doctors were ordered to find a cure. Although they weren't successful, one of them had the great idea of creating false hair. So the first wig was made – from goats' hair – and Louis was so pleased with it that he wore it everywhere, and soon wigs become popular and fashionable all over Europe, even for people *with* hair!

What's this 'ere?

In 1731 an English ship was stopped by Spanish coastguards in the Caribbean and ordered to pay tax. However, the English captain, Robert Jenkins, refused to pay, so they cut off his ear and told him to show it to his king. Jenkins returned to England eight years later and told Parliament what had happened. They were so angry that war was declared immediately, and it became known as the War of Jenkins's Ear.

2 One of these three stories is not true. In your groups decide which story is false.

3 Read through all the stories quickly. Underline the examples of *although* and *however*, and choose the correct word in brackets in this explanation.

Although and *however* are both used to show a connection between two (similar/contrasting) ideas, and they have more or less the same meaning as the word (*and/but*).

(*Although/However*) links two ideas in *one* sentence, and can go at the beginning or in the middle of the sentence.

(*However/Although*) links two ideas in two separate sentences. It usually comes at the beginning of the second sentence.

Unit 22 A SENSE OF HISTORY

4 Work with a partner. Complete these sentences in a logical way.

1. Although they lost the race, ...
2. The illness can last a long time. However, ...
3. Although she wore a wig, ...
4. Part of the town was destroyed. However, ...
5. .... although they never found the gun.

5 Work in small groups. Write a story in the past using all four pictures (about 50–60 words). If possible, use *although* or *however* once. Then read your story to another group.

PERSONAL STUDY WORKBOOK

In your Personal Study Workbook, you will find more exercises to help you with your learning. For Unit 22, these include:

- exercises to help you with link words
- a grammar exercise on passives
- vocabulary revision and word building
- a text about the Russian royal family by someone who saw them just before they died
- a dictation exercise

REVIEW AND DEVELOPMENT

REVIEW OF UNIT 20

1 Personal memories [listening]

A ☐☐ Do smells, tastes and sounds have strong memories for you? Listen to the recording. What memories do the following have for the speakers?

burning wood   cigar smoke
mouthwash   leather   cream
snakeskin   marble

Burning wood reminds the speaker of ...

B Look again at the questionnaire on page 127. Choose two or three things, and tell a partner what they remind you of.

The smell of
The taste of ... reminds me of ... .
The feel of

---

2 I'm sure I'll hear the sea [will and might]

Work in groups. Think about the next 24 hours. Make some predictions which are true for you using the words in the box. Look at the examples first.

Examples: *I'm sure I'll hear the sea.*   *I might see an aeroplane.*
          I think I'll smell perfume.   *I don't think I'll feel cats' fur.*

garlic   cats' fur   a screaming child   fresh paint   a strong wind
a whistle   expensive perfume   an aeroplane   factory fumes   the sea
a spider   the sun on my face   grass   suntan lotion

3 Both and neither [speaking]

Work with a partner. Find five things that both of you can do, and five things that neither of you can do.

Example: *Both of us can drive but neither of us can play chess.*

REVIEW OF UNIT 21

1 What day? What date? [time expressions]

This is a competition. See how quickly you can write down the answers to these questions. When you have finished, put up your hand and shout out 'I've finished'.

1. You are going to Spain on the 20th of next month. What day is that?
2. You are going to the dentist on Thursday week. What date is that?
3. The day before yesterday a friend said to you, 'I'm going to the doctor the day after tomorrow'. What day are they seeing the doctor?
4. You saw a film ten days ago. What day was that?
5. A friend of yours has been in Japan for exactly three weeks. What date did they arrive?
6. You borrowed a book from the library on the first Friday of last month. How many days have you had it?
7. You booked your holiday exactly three weeks ago because you have to book the flight two months in advance. You are going to fly on a Saturday. What date is that?
8. When did you start this exercise?

2 That used to be true [used to + verb]

Read the statements and choose one of these answers:

That's true.
or
That used to be true.

1. The political system in the eastern part of Germany is communist.
2. Japan is one of the world's most important industrial powers.
3. France has a monarchy.
4. Saudi Arabia is the biggest oil producer in the world.
5. Korea is divided into two countries.
6. Iran is ruled by a Shah (king).
7. Britain has an empire.
8. Spain is in the European Union.
9. The President of the U.S.A. is George Bush.
10. The capital of Hungary is Budapest.

Discuss your answers in groups.

23

WHOSE LIFE IS IT ANYWAY?

Language focus:	Vocabulary:
adjectives and adverbs	word building
expressing preferences	social issues
	names and naming

1 Look at the following activities. Which do you find easy to do, and which are difficult, and why? Tell your partner.

- choosing what to wear in the morning
- choosing a new pair of shoes in a shop
- choosing what to eat in a restaurant
- choosing a present for someone in your family

2 Read the text and make three lists:

1. things the person chooses, e.g. he/she chooses to have a shower
2. things the person doesn't choose
3. things in between the two extremes in (1) and (2)

A day in the life ...

Another day dawns as the radio alarm wakes you up at 6.30 in the morning. You get up <u>slowly</u>, knowing that almost everything that will happen today is out of your control. You didn't even choose the radio programme that woke you up – your partner did.

You have a <u>quick</u> shower using the free shower gel you were given at the supermarket last weekend, shave <u>carefully</u>, and put on the clothes your partner so <u>cleverly</u> persuaded you to buy. Then, leaving the house, you get into your company car (the same blue saloon that everyone gets) and drive to the office through the usual traffic jams. At work you are surrounded by colleagues, some very pleasant, but others who drive you crazy. But as you keep telling yourself, you are <u>lucky</u> to have a job at all.

Lunch in the free staff canteen: vegetable soup followed by chicken and chips. You hate

vegetable soup, so you don't eat it; but as the nearest café is a ten-minute walk away, you eat the chicken. During lunch, the boss asks you to stay late tonight for an unexpected meeting. You don't like to refuse because you are planning to ask for a pay rise next week, and you don't want to put her in a bad mood. You work really <u>hard</u> all day and go home. You know you're driving too <u>fast</u> but you don't care. When you get home, the TV is on and the children are watching an endless series of pop programmes and <u>stupid</u> game shows. By the time you have had dinner and the children are in bed, you are too tired to read the <u>interesting</u> book you got from the library at the weekend. Exhausted, you go to bed at 11.00, and your partner tells you to set the alarm for 6.15.

Compare your answers in groups.

3 When do we use adjectives and when do we use adverbs? Discuss these examples with a partner:

*You get up **slowly**.*
*You have a **quick** shower.*

4 Now put the underlined words from the passage into the correct column in the box, and then add the missing adjective and adverb forms. Is there a rule? Are any forms irregular?

adjectives	adverbs
quick	quickly
....	....
....	....
....	....
....	....
....	....
....	....
....	....
....	....

5 Look at the rules for the position of adjectives and adverbs on page 170, and then work with a partner. One of you must put a different adjective into each of these sentences, while the other puts a different adverb.

Example: I left the <u>crowded</u> room.   I left the room <u>angrily</u>.

1. The man drove to the supermarket.
2. The student answered the questions.
3. Did you do your homework?
4. The child ran into the street.
5. He waited for the bus.
6. The teacher opened the door.

Compare your sentences. Try to combine them, making any changes necessary.

Example: *I left the crowded room angrily.*

6 Who chooses these things in your life? Discuss in groups. Here are some expressions you can use:

I choose ... (the clothes I wear.)
I have no choice about ... (the clothes I wear.)
It depends. (Sometimes I choose the clothes I wear.)

1. where you live (the area)
2. where you live (the house/flat)
3. the people you live with
4. the times you get up, eat, work, sleep
5. the clothes you wear
6. the programmes you watch or listen to
7. the way you spend your free time
8. the friends you have
9. what you eat and drink
10. where you sit in class

1 Answer the following questions in groups.

1. How many names have you got, and what are they?
2. Who chose your names, and why?
3. Do your family or friends call you by a nickname? If so, who chose it, and why?
4. Did you have other nicknames when you were a child?

2 Work in groups. Talk about your preferences like this:

I'd rather + verb	*I'd prefer to* + verb
(*I would*)	(*I would*)

Would you rather / prefer to:
- have one first name, or two?
- have one surname or two? (for instance, your father's and your mother's)
- keep your surname or take your partner's surname if you marry?
- have a very long name or a very short one?
- be called by your first name, your surname, or your title in class?
- have your own name or a different one?

Give reasons for your preferences.

3 Read the text. Do you think this woman does a useful job? Discuss with a partner.

She makes $50 an hour choosing names for babies

JO-ANN SAUNDERS has the world's most unusual job – she earns $50 an hour helping parents choose the perfect name for their infant!

'A name creates an image. When you choose a name for your child, you want one that is distinctive, one that makes the child feel good about itself,' advises Saunders. 'But you don't want one that makes him or her feel strange.'

4 ⏍ Here is some more advice. Listen and complete the box.

Jo-Ann's advice	*Examples*
1. *Don't name a child after his father.*	George Foreman
2.	
3.	
4.	
5.	

Compare your answers. Do you agree with Jo-Ann's advice?

5 Work in small groups. Make up suitable, interesting or amusing names or titles in English for the subjects of the photos.

CHOOSING A PARTNER

1 Complete the table on the left while a partner completes the table on the right.

Exchange answers and check them in a dictionary.

Noun	Adjective	Noun	Verb
finance	....	....	choose
religion	....	....	advise
education	....	....	get married
politics	....	....	believe
culture	....	....	compare
society	....	....	get divorced

2 If you choose a partner for life, how important are the following? Complete the table below by putting ticks (✓) in the correct columns.

	very important	quite important	not important
1. Your partner is from the same religion as you.	....	....	....
2. Your partner has similar political views.	....	....	....
3. Your partner is more or less the same age as you.	....	....	....
4. Your partner has similar interests and hobbies.	....	....	....
5. Your partner is from the same country as you.	....	....	....
6. Your partner has a similar financial situation.	....	....	....
7. Your partner has had a similar education.	....	....	....
8. Your partner eats the same kind of food as you (e.g. is not a vegetarian if you eat meat).	....	....	....

Compare your answers in groups.

3 ☐☐ ☐☐ Listen to the recording. The speaker talks about four of the subjects above. Which subjects are they, and what is the speaker's opinion?

4 Look at these questions in groups and choose the ones you want to discuss.

1. Is it a good idea to choose one partner for the whole of your life? Why? Why not?
2. Should children be able to change their names easily at the age of 12? Why? Why not?
3. Should you be able to choose your own doctor? teacher? judge?
4. Should the owner of a company who is planning to retire choose their own replacement?
5. If parents get divorced, should the children be able to choose which parent they live with?

PERSONAL STUDY WORKBOOK

In your Personal Study Workbook, you will find more exercises to help you with your learning. For Unit 23, these include:

- an exercise on adjectives and adverbs
- a pronunciation exercise on sounds and spelling
- several listening passages
- an activity about names and naming
- an opportunity to write about your morning

REVIEW AND DEVELOPMENT

REVIEW OF UNIT 21

1 Weak forms and linking   pronunciation

⟁ Work with a partner. Listen to each sentence, decide how many words there are, then write the number down. (Contractions like *isn't* count as two words.)

2 Relative values   vocabulary

Work alone. Make decisions about the questions below.

Which of these *lasts* longer:
  a cold or flu?
  leather boots or trainers?
  an interesting film or a boring film?
  being married or being engaged?

Which of these *saves* more time:
  using a photocopier or copying by hand?
  a fax or the postal service?
  a food processor or a sharp knife?
  a calculator or an adding machine?

Which of these *takes* longer:
  getting to work or getting home after work?
  putting your clothes on or taking them off?
  spending money or earning it?
  booking a flight or booking a hotel?

Which of these is *worse*:
  a delayed flight or a cancelled flight?
  being in love or being in debt?
  losing your wallet or losing your credit card?
  having to apologise or having to complain?

Add at least one more question of your own to each section. Then discuss your opinions in groups. Ask your group your own questions.

REVIEW OF UNIT 22

1 Did he jump or was he pushed? `passives`

Complete the sentences using verbs from the box, and choose the correct active or passive form.

> die   destroy   invent   throw   become   win   release   arrest

1. Nylon .... in 1935 by Wallace Carothers.
2. The match .... by Italy after a penalty shoot-out.
3. The man .... after a long illness.
4. When the war ended, the prisoners ....
5. He .... Prime Minister after winning the election.
6. Many buildings .... by the earthquake.
7. The woman .... for stealing clothes.
8. Somebody in the crowd .... a bottle at the referee.

2 Think of someone who ... `relative clauses; vocabulary`

Put *who* or *which* in the spaces.

Think of:
– something .... is worn by people with no hair.
– someone .... was assassinated in the 1960s.
– something .... flies, and it sleeps upside down.
– someone .... delivers things to your home.
– someone .... resigned from a job last year.
– something .... was built last year.
– someone .... was elected last year.
– something .... was written in the 19th century.

Now write down an answer for each one.

Example: *Something which is worn by people with no hair.* **wig**

Read out your answers to a partner in the wrong order, and see if your partner can give you the correct question.

Example: A: *A wig.*
        B: *Something which is worn by people who have no hair?*
        A: *That's right.*

24

CINEMA AND THE ARTS

Language focus:	Vocabulary:
present simple active and passive	cinema, theatre
past simple active and passive	music, artistic jobs
present perfect simple	adjectives describing character
be able to + verb; *be good at -ing*	

CREATIVE PEOPLE
vocabulary

1 Complete the following table.
Work with a partner.

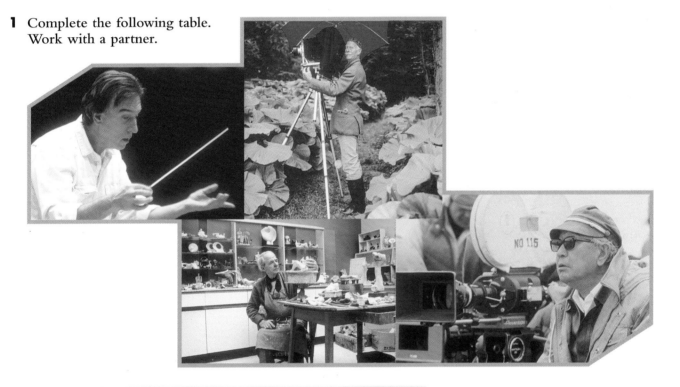

Person	*What they do*	*Example (living or dead)*
novelist	*writes novels*	*John Le Carré*
opera singer	*sings in operas*	*Maria Callas*
painter	....	....
film director	....	....
poet	....	....
composer	....	....
photographer	....	....
musician	....	....
actor	....	....
conductor	....	....
fashion designer	....	....
sculptor	....	....
architect	....	....

Now test each other, like this:

A: *Who's John Le Carré?*
B: *He's a novelist.*

A: *Who was Maria Callas?*
B: *She was an opera singer.*

or

A: *What does John Le Carré do?*
B: *He writes novels.*

A: *What did Maria Callas do?*
B: *She sang in operas.*

2 These three sentences describe the qualities you need for one of the jobs. Which one?

You have to be ...*imaginative*........................ .
You need to be able to ...*describe places and people*........ .
You have to be good at ...*telling a story*...................... .

With a partner, write similar descriptions about one of the other jobs, with the same sentence beginnings. Read them to another pair. Can they guess the job?

3 ⫍⫐ Nickie is a television costume designer and Martin is a holographer. Listen to them talking about other jobs they could or couldn't do, and complete the table.

Nickie	Yes/No		Martin	Yes/No
1. *fashion designer*	*yes*		1. *architect*	....
2.	....		2.	....
3.	....		3.	....
4.	....		4.	....

4 Imagine you could have one of the jobs in Exercise 1. Which one would it be and why? And which would be the worst? Discuss in groups.

Example: *I'd like to be a(n)* .... *because* ....
I'd hate to be a(n) .... *because* ....

1 Look at this statue. What is it?
How could you get one?
Where could you receive it?
Tell a partner.

2 Here are some facts about the Oscar awards. Read the text and try to remember as much as possible. Check any vocabulary you don't know in a dictionary.

1. The Academy was formed in 1927 by Louis B Mayer. The first winners were chosen by five judges.

2. The statuettes have been called Oscars since 1927, when a secretary at the Academy said that they looked like her Uncle Oscar.

3. The statuettes are 34 cm high and cost about $100 to make.

4. Each year, members of the Academy's twelve branches choose five nominations in each category, and the winners are then chosen by the 5,000 members of the Academy.

5. The ceremony has never been cancelled, but it was postponed in 1968 after the assassination of Martin Luther King, and again in 1981 after the attempt to kill Ronald Reagan.

6. The film which has won the most Oscars is *Ben Hur*. It won eleven Oscars in 1959.

7. Woody Allen has won three Oscars but has never been to the ceremony to receive the awards.

8. The youngest ever Oscar winner was Shirley Temple. She received a special award when she was just five years old, in 1934.

9. The oldest winner was Jessica Tandy, who won an award for *Driving Miss Daisy* in 1990, aged 80.

10. If a film wins an Oscar, it will probably earn at least an extra $20m.

3 🎧 Listen to the following questions on the Oscars and write down the answer a, b or c. Close your book before you listen.

Compare your answers with a partner and then look back at the text to see who got the most correct.

4 Without looking at the text in Exercise 2, complete the following sentences putting the verb in brackets into the correct tense. You must choose between:

present simple passive   e.g. *I am given/she is given*
past simple active   e.g. *I gave/she gave*
past simple passive   e.g. *I was given/she was given*
present perfect simple   e.g. *I have given/she has given*

1. The Academy (form) in 1927 by Louis B Mayer, and the first winners (choose) by five judges. Now the winners (choose) by the 5,000 members of the Academy.
2. Every year five films in each category (select) by the members of the Academy's twelve branches.
3. *Ben Hur* (win) more awards than any film since 1927. It (collect) eleven Oscars in 1959.
4. The ceremony (postpone) in 1968 after the assassination of Martin Luther King, and the organisers also (postpone) the ceremony in 1981 after an attempt to kill Ronald Reagan.
5. Woody Allen (win) three Oscars so far, but he has never been to the ceremony.
6. Jessica Tandy (win) an award in 1990 for *Driving Miss Daisy*.

Compare your answers with a partner, and then you can check most of them by looking back at the text.

5 Choose your own Oscar nominations for all time.

Here are the categories: Now choose *one* of the following:

Best film   Best film music
Best actor   Best special effects
Best actress   Best costume design
Best director

Move round the class. Who has similar ideas to you?

CINEMAS AND THEATRES vocabulary

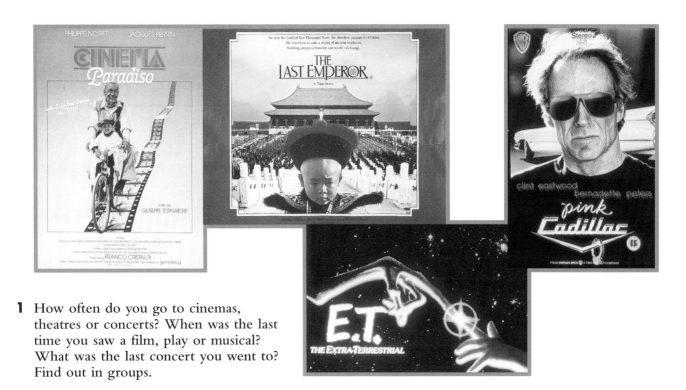

1 How often do you go to cinemas, theatres or concerts? When was the last time you saw a film, play or musical? What was the last concert you went to? Find out in groups.

2 Do we use the following words and phrases to talk about the cinema, the theatre or both? Put the words in the correct column.

stage
to book seats
continuous performance
subtitles
curtain
box office
adverts
aisle
screen
audience
numbered seats
trailers
to clap
dubbing/dubbed
interval

Cinema only	Theatre only	Cinema/Theatre
	stage	

Compare your answers with a partner, and check your pronunciation with your teacher.

3 Answer these questions about cinemas in your town or city.

WHAT ARE YOUR CINEMAS LIKE?

1. Do you think that cinemas are expensive or quite cheap?

2. Is it common to book seats in advance in cinemas?

3. Do you have people who show you to your seats?

4. Are most seats numbered or can you sit where you like?

5. Is there normally a single price for seats, or do you have seats at different prices?

6. Do you normally have continuous performances or is there a break between each performance?

7. Are there lots of advertisements and trailers for future films before the film starts?

8. Are foreign films usually dubbed, or do they have subtitles?

9. Is it common for the audience to clap at the end of a film?

10. Do people usually eat at the cinema during the performance? If so, what?

Discuss your answers in groups.

4 Work in three groups. One group must write six questions about cinema; another group six questions about theatre; and the third group six questions about music. You can use information from the unit if you like. (You must know the answers to your questions.)

Ask the other two groups your questions. Give points for correct answers.

Who won?

PERSONAL STUDY WORKBOOK

In your Personal Study Workbook, you will find more exercises to help you with your learning. For Unit 24, these include:

- an exercise on theatre and cinema vocabulary
- another exercise on the past simple active and passive
- a crossword
- a listening activity about playing in a band
- a pronunciation exercise
- the final page of your visual dictionary – musical instruments, inside a theatre

---

REVIEW OF UNIT 22

1 Contextual guesswork   vocabulary

Using your knowledge of the vocabulary in these sentences, try to guess the missing word. If you know the answer but not the word in English, use a bilingual dictionary.

1. The accident happened around midnight. The car .... into a tree at the side of the road, but fortunately no one was ....

2. Terrorists .... the plane and took over one hundred hostages. After negotiations with the police and airport authorities, they agreed to .... the women and children.

3. When he was sitting with his back to me I didn't .... him, but when he .... and walked across the room, I realised who it was.

4. Soldiers fighting in the .... for control of the town, say that fifty men were killed and hundreds were ....

5. The President was .... by a bomb which .... under his car as he
   was on his way to the airport.
6. The man .... peacefully in bed after a long .... The funeral will
   be held next Tuesday.

2 Past and present | tense revision |

Expand the words below into four true sentences using:

the present simple	Example: *I **live** with my **parents**.*
the present continuous	Example: *My cousin **is living** with her **parents** at the moment.*
the past simple	Example: *My brother **lived** with our **parents** before he got married.*
the present perfect	Example: *I've **lived** with my **parents** all my life.*

1. write/letter(s)   3. work/hard   5. drive/work
2. spend/money   4. have/lunch

REVIEW OF UNIT 23

1 Difficult choices | prefer and rather |

Choose between the pairs of activities below and tell a partner. Make sentences using:

I'd rather + verb
I'd prefer to + verb

Example: *I'd rather eat the caviar.*
   or
   I'd prefer to eat the Swiss chocolate.

1. eat 100g of caviar / eat 100g of Swiss chocolate
2. clean the oven / do a week's ironing
3. lose your wallet / lose your front door key
4. meet the ruler of your country / meet the Secretary General of the United Nations
5. put on 6 kilos / lose a tooth
6. break your ankle / break your nose
7. have a starter and a main course / have a main course and a dessert
8. learn how to make clothes / learn how to fly a plane
9. go skiing / play tennis
10. get rich quickly and die young / be poor and live a long time

2 Hard or hardly | adjectives and adverbs |

Correct the eight mistakes in the text, then compare your answers in groups.

I went to see my hairdresser the other day. I've known him for a long time and he's a
marvellous hairdresser – he cuts hair beautiful. He's always very politely to his customers and
he works hardly and efficiently. People always take their troubles to their hairdresser; Ray just
listens patient and then makes suggestions gentle. He always behaves extremely professional.
I've never had a hairdresser who cuts hair so well; he's quickly and he's never lately.

**Work with a partner. Rewrite the text, changing the job, the adjectives and the
adverbs to describe a completely different person.**

Example: *I went to the dentist's the other day. I've known him for a long time and he's
   a terrible dentist ...*

GRAMMAR REFERENCE

PRESENT SIMPLE

Uses

1. To talk about habits and routines:

   I study every morning.
   She goes to the cinema twice a week.

2. To talk about a permanent situation:

   I like Mozart.
   He works for a large company.

3. To talk about facts which are always true:

   Water boils at 100 degrees centigrade.
   Most birds build nests.

Forms

Positive and negative

I You We They	work. don't (do not) work.
He She It	works. doesn't (does not) work.

Questions

Where	do	I you we they	live?
Where	does	he she it	live?

PRESENT CONTINUOUS

Uses

1. To talk about things happening now, at the moment of speaking:

   Be quiet! I'm working.
   I can see the children – they're playing in the garden.

2. To talk about something which is temporary and happening around now, but not necessarily at the moment of speaking:

   I'm doing a typing course.
   (I started last week and it finishes in two months.)
   They're showing Rambo again at the cinema.
   (It's on this week.)

See also Unit 8 for a further use of the present continuous.

Forms

Positive and negative

I	'm (am) 'm not	
He She It	's (is) isn't (is not)	working.
We You They	're (are) aren't (are not)	

Questions

What	am	I	doing?
	is	he she it	
	are	we you they	

SHOULD

Should can be used to correct things that are wrong:

   *These clothes **should be** in the cupboard, not on the bed.*
   *This form **should have** your signature on it – it doesn't.*

Should is also used for giving advice:

   You should go for a walk; the fresh air will make you feel better.

Note:
Should is followed by the verb without *to*.

QUESTION FORMS

1. Present simple and past simple questions require the verb *do* in different forms. The exception is questions with the verb *be*.

QUESTION WORD	AUXILIARY	SUBJECT	MAIN VERB	....
When	do	you	get up?	
How long	does	it	take?	
Why	doesn't	it	work?	
	Do	you	like	mustard?
Which	do	they	prefer?	
How often	do	you	see	her?
How	did	you	get	here?
How much	did	that	cost?	
Why	didn't	he	come?	

2. With *be*, *have got*, and *can*, you must still remember to put the verb before the subject.

QUESTION WORD	AUXILIARY	SUBJECT	....
	Are	you	busy?
How far	is	the station?	
	Have	you	got any sisters?
What	has	he	got?
	Can	they	swim?
Why	can't	she	do it?

Note:

You cannot have two question forms in one English sentence, so if you begin a sentence with *Do you know*, or *Could you tell me*, the following question must be positive. So:

Where's the bank?	*Do you know where the bank is?*
When do we arrive?	*Could you tell me when we arrive?*
Why did they leave?	*Do you know why they left?*
What are you doing?	*Could you tell me what you are doing?*

3. *What*, *which*, and *whose* can also be followed by a noun:

QUESTION WORD	NOUN	AUXILIARY	SUBJECT	....
Which	way	did	you	go?
Whose	book	is	that?	
What	nationality	is	she?	
What	type of car	has	he	got?
Whose	story	do	you	believe?

4. There are a number of common questions which are important and easily confused:

A: ***What's it like?*** (Tell me more about it/describe it/give me your opinion of it.)
B: *It's quite small, but it's very nice.*

Note:
We don't use *like* in the answer.

A: ***Do you like*** chocolate? (in general)
B: *Yes I love it.*
A: ***Would you like*** some chocolate? (= Do you want some chocolate that I am offering you now?)
B: *No thanks, I only had lunch half an hour ago.*

How do you do? (when you first meet someone)
How are you? (to greet someone you know or have met before)

PAST SIMPLE

Uses

1. To talk about past events and situations which are completed at a specific or known time:
   We saw them a week ago.
   She lived there for ten years. (She doesn't live there now.)

2. To talk about regular or repeated activities in the past, which don't happen now:
   When I was at school, we did homework every night.
   She never spoke to me at work.

Forms

Positive and negative

I		
You	came	
He	didn't come (did not)	
She		yesterday.
We	arrived	
They	didn't arrive	

Regular verbs end in *-d* (arrived) or *-ed* (painted) in the positive form.
See page 175 for the list of irregular verbs.

Questions

Did	he	
	she	tell you?
Didn't	we	
	etc.	

PAST TIME EXPRESSIONS

this morning (if the morning is finished)
this afternoon (if the afternoon is finished)
yesterday
the day before yesterday

last { week / month / year }

two weeks / three months / four years } ago

POSSIBILITY AND PROBABILITY

We use the following expressions:

There	is are might be	definitely probably	a factory. some factories. a bank. some banks.

There	probably definitely	isn't a factory. aren't any factories.

Notes:
1. Notice the position of *probably* and *definitely*: after the verb *to be* in a positive sentence, and before the verb in a negative sentence.
2. Notice that *some* is used in positive sentences with plural nouns (some factories) and uncountable nouns (some bread), but *any* is used in negative sentences. *Any* is also used in questions.

INDIRECT QUESTIONS

See Grammar Reference for Unit 2 Question Forms, note 2.

4

PRESENT PERFECT

Use

To talk about events and situations that happened in the past, but you don't say when they happened:

She has been to Greece twice.
Have you ever worked in a bank?
I've never had a beard.

See also Unit 6 and Unit 14 for further uses of the present perfect.

Form

Positive and negative

	Have/Has	Past participle	
I You We They	've (have) haven't (have not)	painted written	a self-portrait. a book.
He She	's (has) hasn't (has not)	studied	English.

Questions

Have	you they	(ever)	written	a novel?
Has	he she	(ever)	lived	abroad?

See also the list of common irregular verbs at the end of the Class Book.

Contrast with Past Simple

We can use the present perfect and the past simple to talk about things that happened in the past, but when we say *when* these things happened, we have to use the past simple. Compare:

I've worked in Spain.
I worked in Spain two years ago.

She has written three plays.
She wrote three plays before she got married.

Have you ever been to Germany?
Yes, I was there last year.

INFINITIVE OF PURPOSE

Use

To talk about the purpose of an action, or why we do something:

*You can use a newspaper **to kill** flies.*
*I went there **to buy** tickets for the concert.*

FREQUENCY EXPRESSIONS

I	always often quite often sometimes occasionally hardly ever never	go to the cinema on Sundays.

I go to the cinema	every day. once a week. twice a month. every couple of weeks. every other Sunday. three times a year. whenever I feel like it.

Note:
1. The single word adverbs in the first table go between the subject and the verb in positive sentences. The exception to this is with the verb *to be* and modal

auxiliary verbs like *can* and *should*. In this case, the adverb follows the verb:

I am often late.
I can never remember.

2. The expressions in the second table usually go at the end.
3. In negative sentences, *always* comes after the auxiliary verb, but *sometimes*, *occasionally*, and *often* normally come before the auxiliary verb:

*The train doesn't **always** stop here.*
*The train **often** doesn't stop here.*
***Sometimes** the train doesn't stop here.*

REFLEXIVE PRONOUNS

Use

When the subject and object of a verb are the same, we use reflexive pronouns:

She cut herself on the glass.
Mark looked at himself in the mirror.

Form

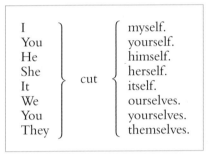

Note:

We don't use reflexive pronouns in English for actions that we normally do to ourselves:

He got up and shaved quickly. (not he shaved himself)
They got dressed and went out. (not they dressed themselves)

but we can use reflexive pronouns in special examples for emphasis:

Today, for the first time, I shaved myself without the nurse's help.
My little girl is learning to dress herself.

6

SHOULD

Use

To talk about what you think is the right or correct thing. We often use this to express our opinions:

I think English lessons should be interesting.
I don't think adult learners should sit in silence in class.

Remember that *should* is followed by the infinitive without *to*.

SO AND *SUCH*

Use

To emphasise adjectives and nouns, often followed by a result clause:

*It was **so** hot that we went to the beach.*
*It was **such** a hot day that we went to the beach.*

Form

You use *so* before adjectives without nouns:

	cold	
It was so	*windy*	*that we stayed at home.*
	horrible	

You use *such* before noun phrases – adjectives and nouns:

such (a/an) + adjective + noun

such a nice day (singular, countable)
such lovely children (plural, countable)
such terrible weather (uncountable)

It was such a nice day that we went out.

PREPOSITIONS + *-ING*

Form

If a verb follows a preposition, it must be an *-ing* form. You cannot use the infinitive:

*They had a cup of coffee **before** leav**ing**.*
***After** finish**ing** her work, she went to bed.*
*Don't go **without** com**ing** to see me first.*
*These apples are not **for** eat**ing**.*

PRESENT PERFECT (2)

Use

In Unit 4, we looked at the form and one use of the present perfect. This tense is also used to talk about actions happening in a period of time which has not finished:

I've met her three times this week.
(This week has not finished.)
She's been to visit them today.
(It is still the same day.)

Compare:

I saw her this morning. (It is now the afternoon or evening: a different time period from now, so we use the past simple.)

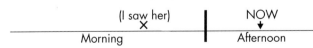

I've seen her this morning. (It is still the same morning, so we use the present perfect.)

Compare:

*I went to Sweden **last** year.*
*I've been to Italy **this** year.*

COMPARATIVE AND SUPERLATIVE ADJECTIVES

Use

Comparatives

To say that something has more or less of something than another thing:

>   *Jeff is **younger than** Jo.*
>   *Paris is **more interesting than** my home town.*

Note:

Than is used when comparing two things.

Superlatives

To say that something has more or less of something than anything in its class:

>   *Jane is **the youngest person** in our group.*
>   *It is **the most exciting book** I've ever read.*

Note:

The is normally used before superlative adjectives.

Forms

ONE SYLLABLE ADJECTIVES

Add *er* to make a comparative;
add *est* to make a superlative:

old	older	the oldest
short	shorter	the shortest

Spelling notes:

1. One syllable adjectives ending in -*e*, add -*r* and -*st*:

wide	wider	widest

2. One syllable adjectives with consonant–vowel–consonant form double the last consonant:

fat	fatter	fattest
big	bigger	biggest

THREE OR MORE SYLLABLE ADJECTIVES

Add *more* before the adjective to make comparatives.
Add *the most* before the adjective to make superlatives.

more expensive	the most expensive
more reliable	the most reliable

TWO SYLLABLE ADJECTIVES

Normally these follow the rules for three syllables:

more boring	the most boring
more useful	the most useful

except:
adjectives ending in *y*, change to *i* and add -*er* or -*est*:

happy	happier	happiest

IRREGULAR ADJECTIVES

good	better	best
bad	worse	worst
little	less	least
much	more	most

CAN AND COULD FOR ABILITY

Use

To talk about ability in the present (*can*) and in the past (*could*):

>   *I can swim quite well.*
>   (= I am able to swim.)
>   *I can't speak Swahili.*
>   *I could read when I was 6.*
>   *He couldn't read or write.*

Form

Can and *could* are followed by the infinitive without *to*.

HAVE TO DO, NEED TO DO, DON'T HAVE TO DO, DON'T NEED TO DO

Use

To talk about obligation and necessity, or no obligation or necessity:

>   *Dentists* have / need *to be good with their hands.*

>   *Bank managers don't* have / need *to be artistic.*

In the negative form, the meaning is that it is *not* necessary.
(It is *not* necessary for bank managers to be artistic, but if they are, that is OK.)
Do not confuse *don't have to* with *mustn't*.
See Grammar Reference for Unit 9 on page 163.

8

WILL

Use

To express a decision to do something, *at the moment of speaking*:

>   A: *Come with us this evening.*
>   B: *I can't. I have to do my homework.*
>   A: *You can do that tomorrow.*
>   B: *Yes, that's true. OK, **I'll come** with you.*

Form

Will (usually the contraction *'ll* or *won't* in the negative) is followed by the infinitive without *to*, and it is the same form for all persons.

I / You / She / We / They	will ('ll) / will not (won't)	take him. / come. / get it.

Note:

For other uses of *will*, see Grammar Reference for Units 16 and 20.

GOING TO

Use

To express a future plan or intention, made *before the moment of speaking*:

I'm going to watch TV this evening.
How long are you going to stay in Australia?
She isn't going to buy any new furniture.

Form

The verb *to be* + *going* + *to* + infinitive

PRESENT CONTINUOUS (For the future)

Use

To talk about a planned future *arrangement*:

I'm having lunch with some friends.
We're meeting them at the cinema at 7 o'clock.

This use of the present continuous is very similar to the *going to* future, and we could use *going to* in all cases. But if the plan includes an arrangement with others, most native speakers often prefer to use the present continuous. For plans that do not include arrangements with others, we use *going to*. Compare:

I'm seeing my uncle this evening.
(It is arranged and my uncle knows about it.)

I'm going to see my uncle this evening.
(It is my plan. My uncle may know about it, or he may not.)

Form

As with all uses of the present continuous. See Grammar Reference for Unit 1.

<hr>

9

PRESENT SIMPLE PASSIVE

Use

When you are more interested in the person or thing *affected by an action*, and not the person or thing *responsible for the action*, you use the passive:

Coffee is grown in Brazil.
(We are more interested in *coffee* than who grows it.)

Tea is served in cups or glasses.
Doctors are trained in hospitals.
Green is made by mixing yellow and blue.

Form

present tense of *to be* + past participle

MODAL VERBS: *SHOULD, MUST, HAVE TO*

Should/Shouldn't

Use

To talk about things which are acceptable or unacceptable, or a good or bad idea:

You shouldn't serve champagne in china cups.
You should wash lettuce before you eat it.

Form

should(n't) + infinitive without *to*

Must/Mustn't

Use

To say strongly that something is necessary (*must*) or unacceptable/not permitted or dangerous (*mustn't*):

You must be a member to get in this club.
You mustn't eat poisonous fruits.

Form

must + infinitive without *to* for all persons (there is no 's' on the third person singular).

Have to/Don't have to

Use

In the affirmative, *have to* is similar in meaning to *must*:

You { *have to* / *must* } *pay for food in shops.*

Some grammar books say there is a distinction between them: *must* is an obligation that depends on the person speaking; *have to* is an external obligation (a rule or a law). We do not think this is important at this stage.

In the negative form, however, *don't have to* has a very different meaning from *mustn't*.
Don't have to means *don't need to*, or *it is not necessary*.
Compare:

You don't have to wear a hat in this building.
(It isn't necessary, but you can if you want to.)

You mustn't wear a hat in this building.
(It is unacceptable or wrong to do it.)

Form

Have to is like *eat*, *go*, etc., and requires the auxiliary *do* or *did* in questions and negatives. It is followed by the base verb:

I
You
We } *have to* *go now.*
They
He/She *has to*

Questions
Do you have to go?
Does he have to go?

Negative
I don't have to go.
He/She doesn't have to go.

10

-ING FORM OR INFINITIVE

When certain verbs are immediately followed by another verb, the second verb is an -ing form. For other verbs, the second verb is an infinitive.

1. Verbs followed by an -ing form
   Some of these are verbs which mean like or hate:

   enjoy
   don't mind
   dislike
   can't stand
   loathe (= hate)
   resent
   detest (= hate)

   Other common verbs followed by an -ing form:

admit	*avoid*	*consider*	*delay*
deny	*finish*	*give up*	*imagine*
involve	*miss*	*practise*	*regret*

2. Verbs followed by an infinitive
   Here are some of the most common examples:

agree	*arrange*	*attempt*	*decide*
expect	*forget*	*hope*	*offer*
promise	*refuse*	*want*	*would like*

3. Some verbs can be followed by an -ing form or infinitive. Often there will be a difference in meaning, but with these four examples, the difference is very small:

   love
   like   *to go …*
   hate   *going …*
   intend

PREPOSITION AND -ING FORM

When a preposition is followed immediately by a verb, the verb is an -ing form:

*She is fond **of** walking.*
*I'm not interested **in** listening to music.*
*They are keen **on** swimming.*

11

ENOUGH/TOO

Use

We use *too* + adjective to say that something is more than we want or need or like, or more than is acceptable:

*It's **too hot** in this room.*
= It is excessively hot.

Too and *very* are sometimes confused. Compare:

It's too hot. (It is excessively hot and I am unhappy about it.)
It's very hot. (This is not necessarily excessive.)

We use adjective + *enough* or *enough* + noun to say that something is sufficient:

*This sofa is **big enough** for three people.*
*Have you got **enough information**?*

Form

Too is followed by adjectives:

They didn't go because they were too busy/tired/young.

Enough comes *before* nouns, but *after* adjectives:

We hadn't enough time/money/plates. (nouns)
They're old/clever enough to know the answer. (adjectives)

TOO MUCH/TOO MANY + NOUN

Use

To talk about something which is excessive:

*There are **too many people** sleeping on the streets these days.*
*Your brother has **too much money**.*

Form

Too much is followed by uncountable nouns:

too much time/coffee/work

Too many is followed by countable nouns:

too many cats/responsibilities/people

ADVERBS OF DEGREE: A LOT, A BIT, ETC.

Use

To talk about how much something is true:

Does the weather affect you?

Yes, it affects me   *a lot.*
                          quite a lot.
                          a bit.

No, it doesn't affect me   *much/a lot.*
                             at all.

CAN FOR KNOWN POSSIBILITIES

Use

Can has many uses. In Unit 11, we use it to talk about things which we *know for a fact* are possible. It means that something is sometimes true:

Skiing can be very dangerous.
= Skiing is sometimes dangerous.

Computers can cost you a lot of money.

12

PAST CONTINUOUS

Uses

1. We use it to contrast a situation over a period of time (what was happening) with an event or action of a shorter duration (what happened):

He was washing his hair when he heard a noise.

He was washing his hair was the situation, or the background to hearing the noise, which was a simple action.

I sat down and ordered a drink. Three men were playing cards in a corner of the room.

The three men started playing before I sat down, and continued after I sat down.

2. We also use the past continuous to describe a scene in a story:

The sun was just setting and people were going home from work.

Form

was/were + present participle

Affirmative

I was
You were } *working.*
He/She was

It was raining.

We were } *going out.*
They were

Questions

Was it raining?
Were they waiting?

Negatives

It wasn't snowing.
We weren't doing anything.

WHILE AND WHEN

When can mean *during that time* or *at that time*:

I met her when I was living in Madrid.
(*when* = during the time when I was living in Madrid)
We were very pleased when the parcel arrived.
(*when* = at that time)

While means *during that time*:

I met her while I was living in Madrid.

You cannot use *while* to mean *at that time*.
While is often (but not always) followed by the past continuous.

UNCOUNTABLE NOUNS

Uncountable nouns only have one form. They do not have a plural form; they cannot be used with a plural verb; they are not normally used with the indefinite article *a* or *an*:

*I asked them for **some information**.*
*Their **advice was** very useful.*
*I've got **too much equipment** here.*

There are some uncountable nouns in English which are countable in other languages. These cause particular problems, and common examples include:

information	advice	travel	luggage
baggage	money	homework	knowledge
furniture	traffic	research	spaghetti
progress	news	machinery	equipment
hair (on your head)			

PLURAL NOUNS

There are some nouns which *only* have a plural form, and must be used with a plural verb. In English, a number of these refer to items of clothing, accessories and tools, as they are made of 'two parts' (for instance, *trousers* have two legs).

*Your **pyjamas are** on the bed.*
*My **sunglasses were** quite expensive.*
*The **scissors are** in the cupboard.*

When we want to talk about a number of these things, we say *some* or *a pair of*:

I need two pairs of jeans.
I bought three pairs of scissors.
I must get some new sunglasses; my old ones are broken.

Here are some common plural nouns, some of which are singular in other languages:

jeans	trousers	shorts	pants	underpants
pyjamas	clothes	swimming trunks		tights
binoculars	scissors	sunglasses		
glasses (you wear)		pliers	handcuffs	

PRESENT PERFECT (3)

Use

In Units 4 and 6 we looked at two uses of the present perfect.
We can also use this form in English to talk about situations and events which began in the past and continue up to the present moment. We often make clear the connection between these two moments using *for* or *since*.

> *She has lived in Tokyo since 1992.*
> *She has lived in Tokyo for a few years.*

This means that she began living in Tokyo in 1992 / a few years ago, and still lives there now.

> *He has shaved every morning since he was 16.*
> *I haven't seen Mary for about 6 months.*

Present perfect and past simple

Compare:

> *She has worked in Rome for ten years. (and still works there)*

and

> *She worked in Rome for ten years. (but she doesn't now)*

When we ask about a period of time up to the present, we use *how long?*

> A: *How long have you known her?*
> B: *About six months.*

How long can also be used to talk about length:

> A: *How long is the wall?*
> B: *About 20 metres.*

FOR AND SINCE

With the present perfect tense, *for* + time expression describes the *period* during which something has or hasn't happened, or been true:

> *I've known her for a couple of years.*
> *I've known her for a very long time.*
> *I've known her for six weeks.*

Since + time expression points to the *first or last time before now* that something has or hasn't happened:

> *I've had this car since last year.*
> *She hasn't been home since Tuesday.*

15

IF SENTENCES WITH PRESENT TENSES

Use

To talk about general truths or rules using *if*, which means (in this case) *every time* or *whenever*.

If you make a mistake,
{
> *you lose a mark.*
> *you can cross it out.*
> *you should change it.*
> *you have to admit it.*
> *tell me.*
> *don't tell anyone.*
}

Form

If + present simple,
    you
{
> *do this.*
> *can do this.*
> *should do this.*
> *have to do this.*
}
> *do this.*
> *don't do this.*

DEFINITE ARTICLE AND INDEFINITE ARTICLE

Use

1. We use *the* before a noun when the listener and speaker know which thing or person they are talking about. When we don't know which one, or it isn't important to know, we use *a/an* (sometimes we may also use *some* or no article).

   I saw a girl in the chemist's this morning.
   (The speaker and listener know *which* chemist's, but so far, the speaker has not defined *which* girl.)

2. We don't use any article with plural nouns and uncountable nouns when we are talking about things in general. Compare:

   I like dogs. (in general)
   I don't like the dog next door. (a specific dog)

   Furniture is expensive. (in general)
   The furniture in their flat is very old. (specific furniture)

Note:

This is an important rule to learn because it is often different in other languages.

3. We normally use *the* before:
   rivers, oceans, seas, mountain ranges, groups of states, groups of islands, cinemas, theatres, museums, hotels.
   We normally don't use *the* before:
   lakes, mountains, people's names, streets, parks, continents and most countries.

Note:

See Unit 15 for examples of all these places.

Form

Articles include the definite article (*the*) and the indefinite article (*a/an*).

The indefinite article is *a/an* followed by singular countable nouns.

We use *an* before nouns which begin with the vowels *a*,

e, i, o; with nouns which begin with the vowel *u* when it is pronounced /ʌ/, e.g. an uncle, an umbrella (but not when it is pronounced /juː/, e.g. a uniform, a university); and before nouns which begin with a silent *h*, e.g. an hour.

With all other nouns the indefinite article is *a*.

HAD TO, DIDN'T HAVE TO, COULD(N'T)

Use

To talk about obligations in the past:

I had to wear a uniform to school until I was 16.
(I had no choice.)

To talk about the absence of obligation in the past:

I didn't have to go to school on Saturday morning.
(It wasn't necessary.)

Form

Positive: (I) *had to* + base verb

Questions: Did (you) *have to* + base verb?

Negative: (I) *didn't have to* + base verb

COULD(N'T)

Use

To talk about things that were permitted in the past:

We could wear make-up to school when we were 16.

To talk about things that were not permitted in the past:

We couldn't call our teachers by their first names.

Form

Could(n't) + base verb

16

WILL

Use

To talk about something in the future we think will happen:

I think they'll all pass the exam.
We'll probably rent another flat by the end of the year.
Do you think it'll rain tomorrow?
I won't be able to finish my homework if I go out.
I don't think they'll enjoy the party without us.

Form

Will (usually the contraction *'ll* or *won't* in the negative) is followed by the infinitive without *to*, and is the same for all persons.

I		
You		take him.
She	will ('ll)	come.
We	will not (won't)	get it.
They		

Note:

For other uses of *will*, see Grammar Reference for Units 8 and 20.

IF SENTENCES WITH WILL AND MAY/MIGHT

Use

To describe the future consequences (or possible consequences) of an action or situation:

If it rains, we'll stay at home.
If it's fine, we'll go out.
If she leaves now, she won't be late.
If she doesn't listen, she won't understand.
If he works hard, he may pass the exam.
They might not come if you don't remind them.
They will be very disappointed if you don't tell them.

Form

If + present tense (positive/negative), $\begin{matrix} will \\ may/might \end{matrix}$ + verb

The *if* clause *or* the main clause may come first in the sentence.

Note:

For other *if* sentences, see Grammar Reference for Units 15 and 19.

17

SO THAT

Use

To introduce the purpose of an action:

I always leave very early so that I miss the rush hour.
I prepare my lessons in the morning so that I can relax in the evening.
I turned off the radio so that I could concentrate.

Form

1. *So that* is followed by a subject and a verb.
2. When the main clause is in the present tense, *so that* is often followed by *can* or *will*. When the main clause is in the past tense, *so that* is often followed by *could* or *would*. (See the examples above.)

Note:

The purpose of an action can be introduced by *to* or *in order to* followed by an infinitive. See Grammar Reference for Unit 4 for details.

OTHERWISE

Use

Otherwise can mean *if not*:

We must go now otherwise we'll be late.
(= If we don't go now, we'll be late.)
I'll write it down in my book otherwise I'll forget.
I always get up early otherwise I miss the bus.

Form

Otherwise is often followed by *will* (but not always).

LOOK AND LOOK LIKE

We use these to speculate or say what we think based on what we can see:

> *She looks French.*
> *She looks like a doctor.*
> *You look tired.*
> *That hat looks like a cake.*

Form

> *look* + adjective
> *look like* + noun

19

IF SENTENCES WITH WOULD AND MIGHT

Use

To talk about improbable or imaginary situations in the present or future:

> *If I won the race, I would be very happy.*
> (The speaker doesn't think that he/she will win the race.)
>
> *If I had a house in the mountains, I would go there every week.*
> (The speaker hasn't got a house in the mountains.)
>
> *He might get married if he met the right person.*
> (He hasn't met the right person up to now, but if he did, it is possible that he would get married.)

Forms

If + past simple, and *would* or *might* + infinitive without *to* in the main clause.

IF	PAST SIMPLE,	WOULD/MIGHT + VERB
	they invited us,	we might go.
If	I were rich,	{ I would give my money to you. I'd give ...
	we didn't have a car,	we wouldn't go out so much.

Note:

1. We use the past simple tense in the *if* clause, but we are *not* talking about past *time*.
2. With the verb *to be*, we use *were* for all persons (If I/you/he/she/we/they were ...).
   In conversation, people sometimes say *If I was rich* or *If he was rich*. (This form is not used in formal English.)

ADJECTIVES ENDING IN -ED AND -ING

We use adjectives ending in *-ing* to talk about something that causes a feeling:

> *The film was boring.*
> *It was an embarrassing situation.*
> *That man was frightening.*

We use adjectives ending in *-ed* to talk about our response to something, or feelings about something:

> *I was bored during the film.*
> *I was embarrassed by the situation.*
> *I was frightened of the man.*

Common adjectives used in this way include:

> *bored / boring*
> *embarrassed / embarrassing*
> *frightened / frightening*
> *shocked / shocking*
> *fascinated / fascinating*
> *depressed / depressing*
> *disappointed / disappointing*
> *surprised / surprising*
> *disgusted / disgusting*
> *interested / interesting*

WILL, MIGHT, WON'T FOR PREDICTION

For a detailed explanation, see Grammar Reference for Unit 16.

SO AND NEITHER

Use

To show that we agree with someone, or to say that the information about us is the same:

> A: *I work in a bank.*
> B: *So do I.*

Both speakers work in a bank.

> A: *I don't like chocolate.*
> B: *Neither do I.*

Both speakers don't like chocolate. (*or* Neither speaker likes chocolate.)

Form

> *so*
> *neither* + auxiliary verb + subject

You use *so* to agree with positive sentences, and *neither* to agree with negative sentences.

The auxiliary verb used in the statement is usually used in the answer:

> A: *I **can** hear birds singing.*
> B: *So **can** I.*
>
> A: *I **can't** swim.*
> B: *Neither **can I**.*

A: *I'm leaving tomorrow.*
B: *So **am I.***

A: *I'm not very busy.*
B: *Neither **am I.***

A: *I've got two sisters.*
B: *So **have I.***

When you cannot see an auxiliary verb (i.e. in simple tenses), use *do*, *does* or *did*.

A: *I **live** in Spain.*
B: *So **do** I.*

A: *I **went** home.*
B: *So **did** I.*

Note:

In informal English, you can also agree like this:

A: *I'm happy.*
B: *Me too. (So am I.)*

A: *I didn't like it.*
B: *Me neither. (Neither did I.)*

USED TO + VERB

Use

To talk about something which happened regularly in the past, or was true for some time in the past, but is different or not true now:

She used to work in a factory when she was young.
There used to be a factory where the library is now.
He used to visit his aunt every week.
I never used to enjoy music, but I do now.

Forms

Positive and negative

I You He/She We They	used to / didn't use(d) to	work in a factory.

Questions

Did	you he she they	use(d) to	work here?

22

THE PASSIVE

Use

When you are more interested in the person or thing *affected by an action*, and not the person or thing *responsible for the action*, you use the passive:

The man was arrested outside his home.
(We are interested in *the man*, and not the person who arrested him.)
The books were sent yesterday.
(We are interested in *the books*, and not who sent them.)

From these examples you can see that the person or thing responsible for the action is often not given. This is because we are probably not interested in them, and sometimes we don't know who or what they are.

Form

The passive is formed by the verb *to be* + the past participle of the verb. The only tense change is to the verb *to be*:

I   *am/was/will be*   + past participle (e.g. *ordered, taken*)

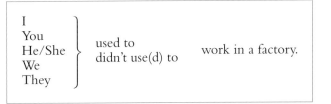

He
She   } *is/was/will be*   + past participle
It

You
We   } *are/were/will be*   + past participle
They

ALTHOUGH/HOWEVER

Both these words are used to link contrasting ideas, and they are similar in meaning to *but*. The difference between them is the way they are used:

1. *He was a big man but he had very small hands.*
   (*But* links the two clauses; there is sometimes a comma before it.)
2a. *He was a big man although he had very small hands.*
2b. *Although he was a big man, he had very small hands.*
   (*Although* can introduce the sentence (b), or link the two clauses (a).)
3. *He was a big man. However, he had very small hands.*
   (*However* is usually used to link contrasting ideas in two different sentences. It is usually followed by a comma.)

REMEMBER + -ING

When we are talking about memories, the verb *remember* can be followed by an *-ing* form. Sometimes the *-ing* form comes directly after the verb, and sometimes it follows an object:

I remember going to Paris as a child.
I remember learning to play the piano.
I can remember my mother telling me stories.
(i.e. I remember now something that happened before.)

The same verb can be followed by an infinitive when it means *not forget*:

> *I remembered to post that letter.* (I didn't forget.)
> (i.e. First I remembered, then I did it.)

Compare these sentences:

> *I remember shutting that window.*
> (I can picture it in my memory now.)
> *I remembered to shut that window.*
> (I didn't forget.)

DEFINING RELATIVE CLAUSES

A defining relative clause identifies a person or thing in the main clause (they are sometimes called identifying relative clauses), and gives us more information about them. These clauses are introduced by a relative pronoun: *who* or *that* for people, and *which* or *that* for things:

> *The woman **who lives in that house** is German.*
> *I lost the book **which he gave me**.*
> *The instructions **which came with the machine** were impossible to understand.*
> *The taxi driver **who took us home** was very friendly.*

Notice that we do not repeat the subject if it is the same in both clauses:

> *The woman who ~~she~~ lives in that house is German.*

23

ADJECTIVES

Use

Adjectives tell you more about a person or thing or state: for instance, age, colour, character. They refer to nouns:

a **brown** book	an **unfriendly** person
boring ideas	a **horrible** smell
She is **kind**.	I was very **busy**.

Word order

Adjectives usually go before a noun:

> *a brown book*

or after verbs like *be, feel, smell, look*, etc.:

> *You look happy.*
> *I'm not rich.*

Two or more adjectives are possible before a noun:

> *I'd like a nice, cool drink.*
> *That's a beautiful old desk.*

Notice that a number of adjectives end in *-ly*, which can be confused with adverbs of manner:

> *lovely   silly   lonely   friendly   daily*

When we want to use these as adverbs, we sometimes use a phrase:

> *He smiled at her in a friendly way.*

ADVERBS OF MANNER

Use

Adverbs of manner tell you *how* something happens or how it is done. They refer to verbs:

> *She drives very **quickly**.*
> (**Quickly** *tells you how she drives.*)
> *He shaved **carefully** and dried his face **slowly**.*
> *The evening ended **happily**.*

Form

Many adverbs of manner are formed by adding *-ly* to the adjective:

> *slow – slowly*

Adjectives ending in *-y* become *-ily*:

> *lucky – luckily*
> *happy – happily*

Hard, fast and *early* are irregular, being the same form for adjective and adverb:

> *She's a hard worker.* (*hard* is an adjective here.)
> *She works hard.* (*hard* is an adverb here.)

(*Hardly* has another meaning: = *almost not*.)

Word order

Adverbs of manner usually come:

> a. after the object:

> *I drank the tea thirstily.*
> *She picked up the money angrily.*

> b. after the verb (or verb + particle):

> *I drank thirstily and sat down quickly.*
> *It was raining hard this morning.*

You *don't* normally put the adverb between the verb and a direct object:

> *He did ~~quickly~~ the exercise.* ^quickly

EXPRESSING PREFERENCES: *WOULD PREFER* AND *WOULD RATHER*

Use

We use *would rather do* or *would prefer to do* when we are saying that we would like one thing or situation more than another:

> A: *Would you like to come for a walk?*
> B: *I'd rather stay at home. / I'd prefer to stay at home.*

> A: *Do you want tea or coffee?*
> B: *I'd rather have coffee, please.*

Form

would rather 'd rather	+ verb	would prefer 'd prefer	to do …
She'd rather go out.		She'd prefer to go out.	
What would you rather do?		What would you prefer to do?	
I'd rather not say.		I'd prefer not to go.	

Note:
If you want to talk about two choices in one sentence, you join them with *than*:

> *I'd rather live at home **than** in a hotel.*
> *I'd prefer to work in a bank **than** in a post office.*

ADDITIONAL MATERIAL

Unit 13 REVIEW AND DEVELOPMENT REVIEW OF UNIT 12: Exercise 2

B Complete the sentences with a suitable verb, phrase or adjective.

1. It was getting .... so I put on my jacket.
2. He's getting very nervous because he's .... his driving test next week.
3. It was getting .... so I turned on the light.
4. It was getting quite .... so I took off my jacket.
5. He doesn't .... birthdays so much now that he's getting old.
6. He was getting .... so I told him to go on a diet.
7. He .... a lot of exercise so he's getting quite fit.
8. It was getting .... and I'm afraid I fell asleep.

Unit 15 GRAMMAR RULES Exercise 3

Text B

We don't usually use
any article before:

streets and parks

Fifth Avenue,
Hyde Park,

....

continents and
most countries

Asia, Spain,

....

We usually use *the* before:

cinemas and theatres

The Lyric Theatre,
the Odeon Cinema,

....

museums and hotels

The British Museum,
the Hilton Hotel,

....

Unit 17 DESCRIBING PICTURES Exercise 4

1. This building is in the Docklands area of London and was once a Victorian water tower. The area was a complex of industrial factories, but these have been converted into flats or offices. This water tower has nine floors and the apartment occupies the top five floors. The style is a 1980s version of the Art Deco style of the 1930s. The dark columns which look like pillars, are actually radiators. This particular room is the kitchen.
2. The room is part of an old renovated house in southern Spain near Mojacar. It is home to two painters – Manuel Conorada and Salvatore Brancaccio – which probably explains why it is full of paintings, sculptures and beautiful furniture. The room in the picture is the first you see as you enter the house, and the statue in the middle is *Mary Magdalena* by Florentine. There is another sculpture of a Spanish bull by Bencurre, and the sofa you see is called a 'chaise longue'.

1. This man knocks on your door and tells you that he lived in your home when he was a boy and he would like to see how it has changed. Would you believe him? Would you let him in?

2. This woman stops you in the street and tells you she has left her purse at home and hasn't got any money for her bus fare. Would you believe her? Would you give her any money?

3. This man, seeing you walking in the rain, stops and offers you a lift. Would you accept? What would you say?

4. This woman is standing outside the front door of a flat. She tells you that she has left her key inside. She wants you to help her break a window to get in. Would you help her? What would you say?

5. This man offers you a hundred dollars for no reason. He tells you that he is rich and doesn't need the money. What would your reaction be? What would you say?

TAPESCRIPTS

Tapescript 1 (Unit 2, Review and development)
1. Is a ruler bigger than a rubber?
2. Can you put papers in a file?
3. If a room is in a mess, is it tidy?
4. Can you read anything on a blank sheet of paper?
5. Can you write something on a word processor?
6. Is *efficient* the opposite of *organised*?
7. Can you drink from a lighter?
8. If you throw something away, do you want it?
9. Can you sharpen something with a dictionary?
10. If you have a break, do you stop working?
11. Do people usually listen to background music?
12. Can you scratch your head?
13. If you are doing a course, do you usually need a notepad?
14. Do people usually revise after an exam?
15. Does your teacher give you housework?

Tapescript 2 (Unit 3, Finding your way)
Version 1
A: So, did you find the hospital OK?

B: Er, not exactly. I came up Holywell Hill as you said, and when I got to the High Street, I went straight across, and I saw the town hall, and turned left, just like you said.

A: No, I didn't say turn left *immediately* after the town hall …

B: Yes, well, that's what I thought you meant. Anyway, I walked along this road – er, Mount Pleasant, I think it was – and I took the second road on the right, but it wasn't Normandy Road. So I stopped and asked an old lady the way, and she told me to go straight ahead, until I got to er Folly Lane, then turn right and take the first turning on my left. And this time it *was* Normandy Road.

A: Oh, well, you weren't very late, and I expect the exercise did you good …

Version 2
MAN: When I got to the station, I remember you'd said turn right.

WOMAN: Mm.

MAN: So I came out of the station and I looked … right didn't seem to be right, but I did turn right and walked up Holywell Hill.

WOMAN: Yeah, yeah.

MAN: Came up Holywell Hill past the information centre which you mentioned. And I got up to the town hall … and the road in front of me didn't sort of look right so I turned left.

WOMAN: What at the town hall?

MAN: That's right. Yeah, didn't you say turn left.

WOMAN: No, you're supposed to go straight on.

MAN: Oh, no. Well, anyway, I turned left which I suppose was my mistake, and I walked up Mount Pleasant Road and got to the end of that and it sort of took a turning down a branch road, then I carried on again and by that time I knew I was on the wrong road because it started to turn into countryside and things.

WOMAN: Are you kidding?

MAN: No. And I thought, oh, no. And I walked on and it … up this other road called, I think it was Hatchwood Drive, I think or something. And there was a golf course there, anyway. So I got to the golf course.

WOMAN: That's miles away!

MAN: Yeah, I found that out. And I got to the golf course and I went in and I phoned for a taxi.

WOMAN: Yeah.

MAN: Because I wasn't going to walk any further around St Albans. A taxi came and got me and I told him where I wanted to go and on the way back we discussed the route and he said you've taken the wrong turning …

Tapescript 3 (Unit 3, Review and development)
1. What's your name?
2. Where are you from?
3. Where do you live?
4. What do you do?
5. Do you enjoy it?
6. Why are you studying English?
7. How do you get to school?
8. What have you got in your pocket?

Tapescript 4 (Unit 4, Review and development)
1. Can you see the street from where you are sitting?
2. Does the room you are in have a carpet?
3. If you open the door of your room, is there another door opposite?
4. If you open the door of your room, can you see any stairs?
5. Can you walk out of your room, turn left and go straight on?
6. Can you walk out of your room, turn right and go straight on?
7. Can you go down a floor?
8. Do you have to go to the next floor to go to the toilet?
9. Can you take a lift to the next floor up?
10. Can you jump out of the window safely?
11. Can you get anything to drink on your floor?
12. Can you phone from your classroom?
13. Can you walk out of your room, along a corridor and out of the building?
14. If you leave the building, do you go past a coffee machine?
15. Do you have to go down some steps to leave the building?

Tapescript 5 (Unit 6, An adult language class)
A: You're studying a foreign language at evening school, aren't you?

B: Yeah, that's right, I'm doing a German course two evenings a week.

A: What's it like?

B: Well, it's really different from when I was at school. I mean, the way people behave is quite different.

A: How?

B: Well, for a start, the teachers were really strict at school – I suppose they had to be; there were thirty of us in the class, and most of us were very lazy. But um in this German class, we call the teacher by her first name, and we we talk to her more like she's our equal. And she doesn't force us to do homework if we don't want to.

Oh, and the classroom itself is very different – like at school, we had to sit at desks, and they were nailed to the floor, so you couldn't really move about at all. And here we sometimes sit in a circle and sometimes in a semicircle, and er quite often we just work in groups, so it's it's much much more flexible. Oh, and the other thing is we get up and walk about a lot too.

A: It sounds a bit of a madhouse!

B: Yes, oh, it can be. Oh, it's not like school; you don't have to sit in silence or put your hand up – here, everyone just shouts out if they know the answer. And er if there's anything you don't understand, you just ask the person sitting next to you, or or the teacher.

A: But you still use set texts, course books, that sort of thing?

B: Yeah – we still have a course book, but we can ask the teacher to teach us something in particular if we want to. Um, like in my class, there's this banker who always wants to know lots of economic vocabulary.

A: But, suppose the other learners in the class aren't interested in that?

B: Well, we're adults – so if we don't want to do something, we don't have to. Or we can at least um tell the teacher we don't want to do it. But most of the time there's a a pretty good atmosphere in the class, apart from a couple of people who often just come in ten or fifteen minutes late and don't even apologise. And that's really annoying because then of course the teacher wastes a lot of time explaining things that the rest of us already know.

Tapescript 6 (Unit 6, Review and development)
1. Is your skin on the inside of your body?
2. Can people walk on their heels?
3. Is your elbow between your hand and your shoulder?
4. Can you put your thumb in your mouth?
5. Can you bend your chin?
6. Are your fingernails at the end of your hands?
7. Is your neck near your toes?
8. Are your knees above your throat?
9. Is your bottom near your ankle?
10. Is your wrist next to your arm?
11. Can you touch your lips with your tongue?
12. Can you hurt yourself with your waist?

Tapescript 7 (Unit 7, Review and development)
1. Have you had an English lesson this week?
2. Have you learnt a new sport this year?
3. Did you see your parents last night?
4. Have you shouted at anyone today?
5. Did you have a dream last night that you can remember?
6. Have you cleaned your shoes this month?
7. Have you refused to do anything this month?
8. Have you moved house this year?
9. Have you wasted any time today?
10. Did you buy a new car last year?
11. Have you learnt a new spelling rule this month?
12. When did you start this exercise?

Tapescript 8 (Unit 8, Review and development)
1. I'm writing to their boss.
2. I mustn't lose the address.
3. We planned the meeting last Tuesday.
4. I always forget how to spell *quite*.
5. Whose handwriting is the easiest to read?
6. It's wetter and warmer than yesterday.
7. He's bigger than me.
8. Which suitcase is heavier?
9. She's sitting down over there.
10. I'm putting on weight, but she's much thinner.

Tapescript 9 (Unit 12, Review and development)
1. Can you wear a jacket potato?
2. If a patient recovers, do they get well?
3. Can you use a bubble bath in a sauna?
4. Do you have communion in church?
5. Is a day off a nice thing?
6. Is gardening an outdoor hobby?
7. If something is delicious, do you like it?
8. Is a stranger someone you know well?

9. Can you put logs on a fire?
10. Is spare time the same as work time?
11. Can you repair a pet?
12. Can you start a car?
13. If something is unexpected, does it surprise you?
14. If you regret something, are you happy about it?
15. If you make a promise, should you keep it?

Tapescript 10 (Unit 18, Organisation)
1.

MARY: Hello.

BOB: Hi, is that Mary?

MARY: Yeah.

BOB: Hello, Mary, it's me.

MARY: Oh, hi, Bob, how are you?

BOB: I'm fine, thanks. And you?

MARY: Yeah, OK.

BOB: Listen, Mary, as you know I'm off to Lisbon next week, and I can't leave Felix with my mother because she's ill. Would it be possible for you to feed him while I'm away?

MARY: Yeah, sure. How long are you going for?

BOB: Ten days.

MARY: Yeah, that's no trouble at all.

BOB: Oh, that's very kind of you, thanks.

MARY: No problem. So where are you staying in Lisbon then …

2.

A: Bardens.

B: Oh, good morning. I wonder if you could help me? I'd like to hire some champagne glasses for the weekend. Is that possible?

A: How many d'you want?

B: About 50.

A: Yeah, that's fine.

B: Great. And how much will that be?

A: There's no charge.

B: Really. That's amazing. But … do I have to leave a deposit?

A: Yes. Twenty pounds.

B: OK. And when could I pick them up?

3.

A: Good morning.

B: Oh, hello. Could I speak to Mrs Howard, please?

A: Yes, speaking.

B: Oh, hello, Mrs Howard, it's John Cudmore from BF here.

A: Oh, hello. How are you?

B: Fine, thanks. I'm just ringing to arrange our meeting.

A: Oh, yes. How about sometime next week?

B: Well, I'm afraid I have to go to Paris tomorrow, and I'll be away till the weekend. But how about Thursday the 24th? Is that convenient for you?

A: Um, let me just look in my diary …

Tapescript 11 (Unit 20, Review and development)
1. Do beards grow on trees?
2. If a man escapes, does he get away?
3. If a shop is crowded, is it full of people?
4. Is *empty* the opposite of *full*?
5. If you complain about something, are you happy?
6. Can you feed a cat?
7. Can you take trousers to a dry cleaner's?
8. Can you put trousers in a diary?
9. Does a meeting often have an agenda?
10. Does a credit card have a number?
11. If you go on foot, do you walk?
12. If you cancel a meeting, does it take place?
13. If you are on your own, are you with other people?
14. If you punch someone, are they happy?
15. Do you open wine bottles with a corkscrew?

IRREGULAR VERBS AND PHONETIC SYMBOLS

Irregular verbs

Infinitive	Past simple	Past participle
be	was/were	been
become	became	become
begin	began	begun
bend	bent	bent
bite	bit	bitten
blow	blew	blown
break	broke	broken
bring	brought	brought
build	built	built
buy	bought	bought
can	could	(been able)
catch	caught	caught
choose	chose	chosen
come	came	come
cost	cost	cost
cut	cut	cut
do	did	done
draw	drew	drawn
dream	dreamt	dreamt
drink	drank	drunk
drive	drove	driven
eat	ate	eaten
fall	fell	fallen
feel	felt	felt
fight	fought	fought
find	found	found
fly	flew	flown
forget	forgot	forgotten
get	got	got
give	gave	given
go	went	gone (been)
have	had	had
hear	heard	heard
hit	hit	hit
hold	held	held
hurt	hurt	hurt
keep	kept	kept
know	knew	known
learn	learnt	learnt
leave	left	left
lend	lent	lent
let	let	let
lie	lay	lain
lose	lost	lost
make	made	made
mean	meant	meant
meet	met	met
pay	paid	paid
put	put	put
read /riːd/	read /red/	read /red/
ride	rode	ridden
ring	rang	rung
rise	rose	risen
run	ran	run
say	said	said
see	saw	seen
sell	sold	sold

Infinitive	Past simple	Past participle
send	sent	sent
set	set	set
shake	shook	shaken
shine	shone	shone
shoot	shot	shot
show	showed	shown
shut	shut	shut
sing	sang	sung
sit	sat	sat
sleep	slept	slept
speak	spoke	spoken
spell	spelt	spelt
spend	spent	spent
stand	stood	stood
steal	stole	stolen
swim	swam	swum
take	took	taken
teach	taught	taught
tell	told	told
think	thought	thought
throw	threw	thrown
understand	understood	understood
wake	woke	woken
wear	wore	worn
win	won	won
write	wrote	written

Phonetic symbols

Vowels

Symbol	Example
/iː/	see
/i/	happy
/ɪ/	big
/e/	bed
/æ/	sad
/ʌ/	sun
/ɑː/	car
/ɒ/	pot
/ɔː/	taught
/ʊ/	pull
/uː/	boot
/ɜː/	bird
/ə/	among
	produce
/eɪ/	date
/aɪ/	time
/ɔɪ/	boy
/əʊ/	note
/aʊ/	town
/ɪə/	ear
/eə/	there
/ʊə/	tour

Consonants

Symbol	Example
/b/	back
/d/	dog
/ð/	then
/dʒ/	joke
/f/	far
/g/	go
/h/	hot
/j/	young
/k/	key
/l/	learn
/m/	make
/n/	note
/ŋ/	sing
/p/	pan
/r/	ran
/s/	soon
/ʃ/	fish
/t/	top
/tʃ/	chart
/θ/	thin
/v/	view
/w/	went
/z/	zone
/ʒ/	pleasure

Stress

Stress is indicated by a small box above the stressed syllable.
Example: advertisement

ACKNOWLEDGEMENTS

Authors' acknowledgements

We must first thank our fellow authors Joanne Collie and Stephen Slater. Their creativity and ideas have been a great source of inspiration to us.

We are also indebted to Gillian Lazar for her detailed and invaluable comments on the final manuscript. For the same reason, our thanks to other readers who commented on all or part of the manuscript: Barbara Duff, Diann Gruber, Susan Garvin, Virginia Garcia, Carol Herrmann, Anthony Nicholson and Antonio Marcelino Campo.

For the piloting we must thank James Dingle, who edited the pilot edition and coordinated this stage of the project.

Friends and colleagues have given us permission to use their ideas and activities – or in some cases just inspired us. We would like to thank Philip Dale, Petrina Cliff, Guilherme Pacheco, Tom Bradbury, Alastair and Toshi Banton, Pat Lane and Roz Canning. And a big thank you to the staff of International House and the London School of English for their continued support and encouragement.

At Cambridge University Press, Kate Boyce has been magnificent in guiding the project through the complex stages of editing and production; without her it would never have happened. We would also like to thank Helena Gomm for her astonishing efficiency and good humour in editing the book; and Nick Newton and Randell Harris for their stylish and original design and production work. And then thanks to the producer of all the recorded material, Martin Williamson, and the actors, the staff at AVP.

Finally, our thanks go to our commissioning editor, Peter Donovan, who set the whole thing in motion, and to the rest of the staff at Cambridge University Press.

The authors and publishers would like to thank the following institutions and teachers for their help in testing the material and for the invaluable feedback which they provided:

University of Canberra TESOL Centre, Belconnen, Australia; Queensland College of English, Brisbane, Australia; Waratah Education Centre, Manly, Australia; Insearch Language Centre, UTS, Sydney, Australia; Centro Linguistico di Ateneo, Parma University, Parma, Italy; International House, Turin, Italy; The Cambridge School, Verona, Italy; Languages International, Auckland, New Zealand; Cambridge English Studies, La Coruña, Spain; Dilko English, Istanbul, Turkey; Chichester School of English, Chichester, UK; Regent Hove, Hove, UK; Newcastle College, Newcastle, UK.

The authors and publishers are grateful to the following copyright holders for permission to reproduce copyright material. While every endeavour has been made, it has not been possible to identify the sources of all material used and in such cases the publishers would welcome information from copyright sources. Apologies are expressed for any omissions.

p. 8: the BBC for remarks ascribed to Jeffrey Archer and Sally Beauman from 'The Late Show'; p. 24: material adapted from *Creativity and Intelligence: Explorations with gifted students* by Getzels and Jackson, © J. W. Getzels; p. 24: material adapted from *Modes of Thinking in Young Children* by Michael A. Wallach, Nathan Kogan, © Holt Rinehart and Winston Inc.; p. 24: material based on *De Bono's Thinking Course* by Edward De Bono, © BBC Enterprises Ltd.; p. 33: *The Guardian* for the extract from 'A painful job which has to be done' by Caroline Richmond, © *The Guardian, 1990*; p. 45: *The Independent* for the extract from 'The write stuff' by Fiametta Rocco, 20 October, 1991, © *The Independent* 1991; p. 64: Longman Group UK Ltd for the definition of *enjoy* from *Longman Active Study Dictionary*; extract from *Collins COBUILD Essential English Dictionary* © William Collins Sons and Co Ltd 1988 included with the permission of HarperCollins Publishers Ltd; p. 65: Pan Books Ltd for the poem from *The Happiness Book* by Danny Danziger; p. 67: Catherine Houck for the extract from 'Drug Free Guide to Mood Control', 27 October, 1987, © Catherine Houck, which originally appeared in *Woman's Day*; p. 74: *The Independent* for the extract from 'If it's a beef sandwich' by Janette Marshall, © *The Independent*; p. 78: Heinemann Publishers (Oxford) Ltd for the extract from *Madeleine* by C. Roberts; p. 80: extract from 'Sign of the Dove' published by permission of *The Observer* © 4 November, 1990; p. 82: Mary Glasgow Publications for the extract by Wendy Cope which appeared in *Practical English Teaching*, March 1991, © Mary Glasgow Publications Ltd, London; p. 85: Longman Group UK Ltd for the definition of *weather* from *Longman Active Study Dictionary*; extract from *Collins COBUILD Essential English Dictionary* © William Collins Sons and Co Ltd 1988 included with the permission of HarperCollins Publishers Ltd; p. 90: *National Enquirer* for the extract from 'Brothers reunited after 67 years', 13 October, 1992, © *National Enquirer*; p. 103: Barclays Bank for the questionnaire based on a Customer Service Questionnaire issued to Personal Customers of Barclays Bank plc September 1992, © Barclays Bank; p. 106: *The Independent* for the extract from 'Job opportunities for bright old things' by Dina Rabinovitch, 2 October, 1991, © *The Independent* ; p. 121: *The Guardian* for the extract from 'The Mysterious Hitchhiker', 3 September, 1991, © *The Guardian*; p. 128: *The European* for extract © *The European* 1991; p. 131: *Practical Health* Magazine for extract © *Practical Health* Magazine; p. 141: *National Enquirer* for the extract from 'Wacky ways kids rewrite history' 30 July, 1991, © *National Enquirer*; p. 142: extracts from *Horrible History* by Tim Wood and Ian Dicks, © Simon & Schuster Young Books, reproduced by permission of Simon & Schuster Young Books, Hemel Hempstead, UK; p. 147: *National Enquirer* for the extract from 'She makes a whopping $50' 13 August, 1991, © *National Enquirer*; p. 153: *The Observer* for the extract from 'Low Down: more than 20 things you'll need to know about the Oscars', 1991, © *The Observer*.

The authors and publishers are grateful to the following illustrators and photographic sources:

Illustrators: Veronica Bailey: p. 77; Gerry Ball: p. 46; David Barnett: p. 78; Kathy Baxendale: pp. 20, 29 b, 45, 85, 116; Ken Brooks: p. 26 b; Chris Burke: p. 30; Peter Byatt: p. 16; Paul Dickinson: pp. 15, 41, 129; Darren Diss: pp. 27, 121; Richard Eckford: p. 38; Max Ellis: p. 63; Philip Emms: p. 12; Spike Gerrell: p. 31; Tony Healey: pp. 29 t, 110; Sarah Jowsey: pp. 60, 119; Terry Kennett: p. 59; Joanna Kerr: pp. 40, 69, 84, 98, 115, 171; Vicky Lowe: p. 140; Amanda MacPhail: pp. 24, 35; Cathy Morley: p. 26 t; Pete Neame: pp. 102, 142; Diane Oliver: pp. 13, 71; Liz Pichon: p. 136; Tracy Rich: pp. 18, 114, 143; Eric Smith: pp. 104, 105; Phillip Tyler: p. 58; Emma Whiting: pp. 117, 149; Alison Wisenfeld: pp. 80, 145; Celia Witchard: pp. 51, 97, 156.

Photographic sources: Ace Photo Agency: pp. 9 l (photo Paul Thompson), 9 tcl (Roger Howard), 10 (Marka), 32 l (Roger Howard), 32 cl (Paul Thompson), 34 (Ian Spratt), 120 tc (Colourstock) and 132 tcr (Kevin Phillips); Adams Picture Library: pp. 25 tl and 52 r; Aquarius Picture Library: p. 154 tc; Art Directors Photo Library: pp. 19 r and 32 r (J King); Estate of H. M. Bateman/Heather Jeeves Literary Agency: p. 95; Jurek Biegus: p. 134; John Birdsall Photography: pp. 21 t and bcl, 52 r, 99 tc, 120 l and bcl and 132 bcr; Anthony Blake Photo Library: pp. 65 tr, 127 l and r; Bridgeman Art Gallery: Millais, *The Huguenot*, p. 76; Britstock IFA: pp. 11 (DIAF), 32 cr (Weststock/B. Drake), 39 (Comet), 52 br (B. Ducke), 70 tc (Zscharnack) and 120 br (G. Schorm); Bubbles Photolibrary: p. 120 r (dentist H. Robinson); BUPA: p. 33; Camera Press: p. 151 tc and bc (Gemma Levine); Al Charaf: p. 90 l, the photograph of Buddy Robinson; Bruce Coleman: pp. 128 l and 148 bcr; Comstock: p. 52 l; *Daily Express*: p. 112 b (John Rogers); Luiza Danza: page 21 t; Timothy J. Gonzalez: p. 90 r, the photograph of Bill Robinson; Greg Evans International: p. 20; Garden Picture Library: p. 65 tl (Michael Howes); Ronald Grant Archive: pp. 153 t and b and 154 l and r; Robert Harding Picture Library: pp. 19 l (Gavin Hellier) and 65 br; Houses and Interiors Photographic Features Agency: pp. 109 (*Be Creative* Magazine) and 112 tr; Geoff Howard: pp. 62 r and 96 t; Image Bank: pp. 62 bc (G. V. Faint), 92 tl, 92 cl (Gio Barto), 92 bl, 96 b (Infocus), 120 cr (police officer), 120 bc, 125 (Peter Turner), 127 c, 132 r (R. Romanelli), 135 t (B. Mitchell), 135 br (D. Vance), 148 tc (Walter Bibikow), 148 bcr (J. Enfield) and 172 (no. 2); *The Independent*: p. 106 (Howard Barlow); Life File: pp. 25 bl (Mike Maidment), 92 tr (Ron Gregory) and 107 b (Tim Fisher); Little Brown, *London Revealed*, John Freeman: pp. 111 and 112 tl; Jim Merrett: p. 99 tr; Moviestore Collections: pp. 154 bc and 155 r; The National Gallery, London: p. 72 t, Turner, *Rain Steam and Speed – The Great Western Railway, bc*, van Gogh, *A Cornfield, with Cypresses* and br, Corot, *The Leaning Tree Trunk*; Network Photographers: p. 99 cl (Martin Mayer); Christine Osborne Pictures: p. 62 tc; Performing Arts Library: p. 151 l; Pictor International: pp. 64 bcl, 124 t and 148 r; Pictures Colour Library: pp. 32 t, 52 tl and 65 bc; Reflections Photolibrary: pp. 99 bc and 104; Retna Pictures: pp. 39 c (M. Putland), 52 bl (Kurt Hardi), 70 l, bcl and bcr (M. Putland), 107 t and c (M. Putland), 132 l, tcl and bcl (Jenny Acheson) and 135 bl (B. O'Sullivan); Rex Features: pp. 151 r and 153 c; RMS: p. 17 (no. 2) for the photograph from Sorbothane ad; Russia and Republics Photo-library: p. 62 l; © Stockfile: p. 17 (no. 3) (Steven Behr); Tony Stone Images: pp. 9 tcr (P. and K. Smith), 9 r, 9 bcl (Bruce Ayres), 39 (Arthur Tilley), 52 cl (R. Passmore), 52 cr (Janet Gill), 64 tcl, 65 tc (Philip Silcock), 65 bl (Reinhard Siegel), 79 l (Peter Correz) and 79 r (Chris Harvey); Telegraph Colour Library: p. 36 r; Topham/Picturepoint: pp. 64 tr, l, tcr and r (Korean girl and man wearing hat), 92 tc, 123, 124 c and b, 148 l and 172 (nos. 1, 4 and 5); Travel Ink: pp. 15 (Derek Allan); John Walmsley Photo-library: p. 36 l and c; David Willen: p. 29; E. C. De Witt & Company Limited:

The photographs on pp. 6, 8, 9 br, 17 bl, 21 l, tcr, r and bcr, 25 (background), 50, 54, 64 bcr (vacuuming), 70 t and br, 74, 83, 87, 89, 99 tl, 122, 128 c and r, 130, 152 and 172 (no. 3) were taken by Peter Lake.

t = top, *b* = bottom, *c* = centre, *l* = left, *r* = right

Design by Newton Harris
Picture research by Marilyn Rawlings
Recordings produced by Martin Williamson, Prolingua Productions at Studio AVP, London

The authors and publishers are grateful to the following for permission to reproduce photographs on the cover:

Image Bank: l (Larry Dale Gordon) and r (Kim Steele); Tony Stone Images: tc (Rainer Grosskopf), bc (Donald Nausbaum) and inset right (Frank Cezus).